CREATIVE WINE COOKERY

By Roy Ald

Illustrations by Loretta Trezzo

An extremely versatile cookbook author, Roy Ald's most recent books include a previous Pyramid gift edition, *Casseroles by Candlelight*, as well as *The Complete Soup Cookbook*, *The Side Dish Cookbook*, *The You-Don't-Have-to-Be-French-to-Cook-French Cookbook*, and *Favorite Recipes of Famous Men*. A board member of the *Société des Gourmets Internationales*, he is also the originator of a syndicated cooking column.

Loretta Trezzo's artistic talent and versatility are apparent in the dozens of cookbooks, decorating and handicrafts books she has illustrated. A graduate of Pratt Institute, she is also a popular designer of book jackets. After having traveled extensively in Europe and the Orient, she and her husband, also an artist, now spend their free time in pursuit of antiques to furnish a country home.

CREATIVE WINE COOKERY

A PYRAMID GIFT EDITION
First printing, October 1972
Copyright © 1972 by Roy Ald
All Rights Reserved. Printed in the United States of America.
ISBN 0-515-09330-0

Cover design by Richard D. Smith

▲ Pyramid Books are published by Pyramid Communications, Inc. Its trademarks, consisting of the word "Pyramid" and the portrayal of a pyramid, are registered in the United States Patent Office. Pyramid Communications, Inc., 919 Third Avenue, New York, N. Y. 10022.

Contents

For more Wine Chef's creations, please turn the page

PRELUDE

The French have long believed that "a meal without wine is like a day without sunshine." Wine, the peerless nectar of the revered grape, has graced both peasant kitchens and the dining tables of the aristocracy for centuries. A festive celebration would never be the same without the effervescent sparkle of champagne. A bottle of wine on the dinner table encourages conviviality, leisurely conversation, the unharried savoring of the meal. Icy *vin rosé*, lovingly lifted from the wicker basket along with the cold chicken, fruit, and cheese, elevates the plebeian picnic to the *haute* "piquenique." And what more elegant finale to a company dinner than a bowl of hot walnuts, or perhaps a chunk of exceptional cheese and a decanter of fine old port?

The Bible instructs us to "eat thy bread with joy, and drink thy wine with a merry heart. . . ." And as anyone who has practiced wine cookery realizes, the special alchemy of this time-honored fluid extends beyond the wine glass into the pot itself. Far more than just another flavoring, it blends with the other ingredients to effect a unique "marriage of flavors" in even the most simple dishes, as it also does in such culinary classics as *Coq au Vin* and *Boeuf à la Bourguignonne*. The alcohol content actually evaporates in the cooking, with a resultant enhancement and diffusion of the flavor. But more than that, wine is the exciting catalyst of cookery which imparts to the prepared dish an inimitable essence that is more than the sum of its ingredients. So that to cook with wine is a culinary adventure unlike any other, promising surprise, delight, and immeasurable satisfaction to both the wine chef and his favored guests.

This book has been prepared by one who has long and lovingly labored to harvest the pleasures of "the kitchen vineyard," and it is dedicated with affection to those who would share the same unrivaled culinary experience.

A Word to the Wine-Wise Chef

Wine cookery was never intended to be shrouded in mystery and reserved for the great chefs of *la haute cuisine*. It is something to be enjoyed every day and in relation to the most ordinary of meals — as well as in those more elaborate preparations one enjoys offering to special guests. Those who intimate that its use imposes a delicate hit-or-miss precision are simply being pretentious, for wine may be added as one might, say, add a pinch of thyme or tarragon to the chicken pot without undue anxiousness. Acquiring a basic knowledge of wines, their use in the cooking and the serving of a meal, is quite uncomplicated even for the novice. But as exhilarating as this happy discovery may be to the initiate, the world of wine is one that encourages further explorations, new ventures of infinite variety, which never lose that first blush of delight.

The pages that follow will serve as an introduction to the essentials of wines and wine cookery and adeptly show the way to transforming easily digestible theory into pleasurably palatable practice. And those who have already ventured beyond the preliminaries on this merry culinaire's journey will find this book to be a happily concise Baedeker for quick and accurate reference — in contrast to many of the formidable massive volumes on the subject. This is indeed a "short and sweet" version to confirm the aphorism that "enjoyment is the signal virtue of the splendid chef."

The Vocabulary of Wine

AGE: This refers to when a wine is at its best. Some are meant to be "drunk young" — that is, shortly after the bottling (sometimes even as soon as within a few months), while other wines may require several years of aging before they attain their peak of readiness for maximum enjoyment. Some of the wines to "drink young" are Beaujolais, Beaune, Chablis, Pouilly-Fuissé and Pouilly-Fumé, rosé, Neuchâtel, Soave, most of the California wines. A few wines which necessitate longer aging in the bottle are the great red Burgundy, Bordeaux, and Rhône wines.

APPEARANCE: a check of the wine's color and clarity, usually by holding a glass by its stem to the light. Any cloudiness or muddiness is undesirable. To oenologists (wine experts), each wine has its own "true" color.

AROMATIZED (AROMATIC) WINES: Wines, both dry and sweet, to which certain herbs and flavorings have been added. Generally served as apéritifs, they include the well-known vermouth, Dubonnet, Cinzano, etc. (See also *Apéritifs*.)

BODY: the substance or consistency of a wine . . .
    light-bodied: delicate, "thin." Also referred to as "light."
    full-bodied: more substance, "heavier" consistency, stronger in bouquet and flavor.

Generally speaking, the young wines are light-bodied, the older ones full-bodied.

BOUQUET: the composite aromas and fragrances of a wine — the second step (after appearance) in the evaluation and full enjoyment of a wine, which one sniffs as a prelude to sipping.

DRY: not sweet. *Sec* in French, except when in reference to champagne, in which case *brut* is the driest and *sec* means sweet.

DECANT: to pour wine from its bottle into another container (called a decanter or a carafe) in order to remove sediment in an aged red wine. Sometimes done to improve the bouquet and flavor of young red wine. White wine is seldom decanted. Be forewarned that some restaurants serve inferior wine *en carafe* so that the labeled bottle will not be seen by the diner.

FORTIFIED WINES: These are wines which have been increased in alcoholic content by the addition of grape spirits. They include sherry, port, Madeira, and others, both dry and sweet, and are also referred to as apéritif or dessert wines (depending on how they are being served).

FRESH/FRUITY: a lively, pleasant "fruitlike" fragrance and taste, generally to be found in good young wines — light whites and reds, as well as rosé. When this quality is lost after too-long aging, the wine is described as "tired" or "flat."

MELLOW: "soft," luscious, "ripe"-tasting, sometimes a little on the side of sweetness.

SPICY: a special, quite agreeable, piquant flavor and aroma. Usually found in white German or Alsatian wines like Traminer, Gewürztraminer.

VINTAGE: this literally means "year" — and in the world of wine, refers to the year in which the grapes were harvested and from which a specific wine was produced. However, it has more commonly come to mean a wine of excellence — as when people say, "a vintage wine." If climatic and other conditions during a given year were ideal, chances are the resultant wine will be a great one —

although there are exceptions when a "bad year" will produce a fine wine, and vice versa. Evaluating wine according to vintage can become a most involved preoccupation and is generally reserved for the more serious connoisseurs. But if such is your inclination, any good wine encyclopedia and/or your wine merchant will serve as a guide.

It should be noted that attention to the vintage is most often paid to the wines of the Burgundy and Bordeaux districts of France. And it is generally agreed that when purchasing wines from northern California — where many of the wineries produce highly commendable ones — there is little, if any, need to be concerned about vintage because of the region's usually stable, agreeable climate.

"Vintage port" refers not only to port that has been made from the grape harvest of the same year but is no less than ten, and no more than fifty, years old.

Knowing the year will also serve as a guide as to *when* the wine should be drunk to be enjoyed at its best. In other words, if a wine is meant to be "drunk young," you would not want to open a bottle labeled with a date many years prior.

GUIDE TO DINING WITH WINE

Bordeaux Burgundy Rhine, Moselle Franconia Chianti Champagne, Sparkling Wine

Which wine to serve with which food ought not to be an intimidating question but rather an invitation to transform the routine meal into an occasion for delight. Spaghetti and meatballs become redolent of "that great little Italian restaurant — remember?" when accompanied by a straw-covered flask of Chianti. Leftover cold chicken becomes a lovely summer luncheon if paired with a bottle of chilled rosé. A late-evening snack of cheese and crackers suggests a bit of Parisian ambience when coupled with a glass of Burgundy or Bordeaux. And so it goes . . . on up to the summit of dining elegance in the tradition of *la haute cuisine*, with each course accompanied by a different, painstakingly selected *vin extraordinaire*.

One need not be a member of an elite society of professional gourmands — experts on vintage years, the great *châteaux*, the *premiers grands crus* — in order to derive deep-felt pleasure from the vintner's liquid magic. When dining very informally at home, an inexpensive *vin ordinaire* need present no problems: white wine with fish, shellfish, and poultry; red with meat, rosé with just about anything. Those iconoclasts who disregard all tradition and prefer to stick solely to personal preference have their right. As do even the enthusiastic aficionados of Cold Duck or apple wine or the brightly labeled concoctions from southern California. The purists can play their stuffy games of unvarying precision if they choose but, in the final analysis, all is fair in love and wine. For the key word is *enjoyment* — if it suits your taste and that of your guests.

But it can be a profound disappointment to spend hours preparing an intricate curry, for example, serving with it your finest wine, and realizing too late that so highly spiced a dish would have been better off with beer. Or to fuss over an elaborate, rich dessert, splurge on a celebrated *brut* champagne, then find that the sweetness of the former makes the latter taste thin and sour. Or to overpower the delicateness of your favorite lobster-in-cream recipe with a heavy red Burgundy or, conversely, to despoil the utter delight of a chilled Chablis by serving it with steak *au poivre* or barbecued lamb chops.

For those, then, who wish to venture into the myriad pleasures of artfully pairing good food with the most complementary wines, herewith a few suggestions, with a bow to some of the more venerable traditions . . .

Wine-Serving Temperatures

Red wines:

Tradition maintains that they be served at "room temperature." But this tradition, having originated in Europe, is not always applicable to America, where homes are generally much warmer. Sixty to 65 degrees ("cool room temperature") is suitable — certainly never above 70°! If necessary, red wine may be briefly chilled (about 20 minutes) on the bottom shelf of the refrigerator — though if it is kept in a wine cellar at, say, 50°, it must never be heated artificially. Many Americans prefer their red table wines lightly chilled (especially in warm weather) and this is perfectly all right for the unexceptional wines. *Sparkling* Burgundy, however, is best nicely chilled.

White wines:
Dry white wines are served chilled; two to three hours in the refrigerator is sufficient. The sweet dessert whites (a Sauternes, for instance) are served even colder and may require about four hours' refrigeration. Champagne should be served very cold indeed.

Rosé:
Serve well chilled.

Sherries:
The dry ones, usually served as apéritifs, are best slightly chilled. The sweeter dessert sherries are served at "cool room temperature."

Vermouth:
Served as apéritifs, dry (French) *and* sweet vermouths are generally chilled.

After-dinner Wines:
Port, Málaga, Madeira are served at "cool room temperature" or slightly chilled, if you prefer.

An Aside on Vin Rose

Do not assume, as so many do, that serving a rosé is always the perfect compromise when in doubt about the appropriate wine.

Vin rosé should not be relied upon as an "all-purpose" wine. It is not, first of all, suitable for a formal dinner. It *is* a delightful picnic and luncheon wine, a happy companion to many light meals, a joy in summer. It is the perfect accompaniment to cold chicken and other cold dishes, nice with ham that is being served with something sweet like pineapple or a sugary glaze, and is often enjoyed with cold lobster. But when serving a fine meal to your guests, it is far wiser to make all that effort worthwhile by selecting the most complementary wine rather than always "settling for" the allegedly all-purpose rosé.

When dining out in a restaurant, the host frequently orders a bottle of rosé, believing this to be the only solution when each diner has selected a different main course. Far nicer, however, to order two *half* bottles (one red, one white) to better complement the guests' choices when they include, say, fish *and* roast prime ribs.

The Serving of Wine

Generally speaking, dishes made with wine should be accompanied by the very same wine at table. There *are* a few exceptions: seafood in a sherry-flavored cream sauce, for example (which would call for a white wine, not a sherry); a brown sauce made with white wine but meant for roast beef or steaks; or perhaps a baked ham that was basted with port (port is not served with the main course) . . . and so on. Such exceptions are few, however, and this section will serve as a helpful guide. Remember, too, that the recipes in this book are followed by suggested wines for using in, and serving with, that dish.

If you are serving more than one wine with the meal, here is the traditional rule-of-thumb: dry before sweet, white before red, light before heavy, young before old, good before exceptional. If only one wine is to be served, it is dictated by the main course.

The richer or "heavier" the food, the fuller the wine. For example, a simple roast or broiled chicken would not call for as full-bodied a wine as one prepared in a rich sauce.

Aperitifs

Generally speaking, an apéritif refers to any drink taken before a meal. However, most people exclude from this category drinks made with hard liquor. And lovers of good food maintain that cocktails before dinner are inappropriate because they dull the taste buds and thus diminish full enjoyment of a fine meal. So that, more specifically, as an agreeable prelude, apéritifs are wine — whether chilled champagne (considered by many to be the greatest apéritif of all); the aromatic wines (vermouth, Dubonnet, Byrrh, Lillet, St. Raphaël, Cinzano, and Campari, to name a few of the better-known ones); or fortified wines (dry sherry, Madeira, port).

Dry red or white wine is frequently served in a tall glass, with chilled club soda, ice cubes, and a spiral of lemon or orange peel. The aromatic wines may be enjoyed in one of several ways: straight; chilled; on the rocks; with a splash of soda; mixed with ice, then strained into a cocktail glass.

Vermouth Cassis is a popular wine apéritif made with dry white vermouth, a few drops of *crème de cassis* (a French liqueur of black currants and brandy), a strip of lemon peel, and sometimes a splash of soda. *Kir* is a variation of this drink in which you substitute chilled dry white wine for the vermouth and omit the soda.

Hor d'oeuvres

Chablis is traditional with shellfish, particularly oysters. Champagne with caviar, also good with smoked salmon. A dry white Burgundy or Riesling with *pâté*. *Quiche Lorraine*, with an Alsatian wine like Traminer. Antipasto, asparagus *vinaigrette*, and other dishes prepared with vinegar will ruin the taste of a good wine. So too with seafood-cocktail sauce, as it tends to overwhelm. Egg dishes (such as the popular Eggs *à la Russe*) also tend to be uncomplementary to wine.

Soups

No wine is necessary with the soup course, particularly with cream soups and bisques. Clear soups and consommés at a formal meal are often served with a dry *amontillado* sherry or Madeira, and the latter is classic with green turtle soup. When a chowder or thick soup (like *bouillabaisse*) is the main course at an informal meal, then the predominant ingredients will dictate the wine selection.

Fish & Shellfish

Dry white wine is the general rule (except when the fish has been cooked in red wine). As mentioned above, Chablis is traditional with oysters and shellfish, though other light young wines are suitable — such as Muscadet or Italian Soave, or a domestic Chardonnay. Pouilly-Fuissé and Pouilly-Fumé are lovely with simple fish dishes, as are the Alsatian and California Rieslings. Mosels and

Rhines, Sancerre, in addition to those listed above for shellfish. For strong-flavored fish and for seafood in cream sauces, try the fuller-bodied dry white wines, like a Meursault or Montrachet, a German Rheingau, many of the Graves, California's Chenin Blanc. For very informal meals, an inexpensive choice might be the California Mountain White. For fish cooked in red wine, such as salmon, you may wish to try a Beaune or a red Chassagne-Montrachet.

Poultry

White wine is generally served with chicken, though there are exceptions. *Coq au Vin*, for instance, is cooked in red wine and therefore served with one. Roast chicken goes nicely with a red Beaujolais. So too with roast turkey: while it goes well with such white wines as Pinot-Chardonnay or Dry Semillon from California, or a Puligny-Montrachet, a fine red Bordeaux will accompany a holiday bird with distinction. Chilled rosé is a lovely accompaniment to cold sliced chicken and turkey. Poultry prepared in a rich sauce is best complemented by the fuller-bodied white Burgundies, or a Graves, or a dry California Sauvignon. Chicken in an Italian-style tomato sauce calls for an Italian red. Roast duck (including *à l'orange*) is complemented by either a good white Burgundy or red Bordeaux. A more "ponderous" recipe, perhaps a ballottine of duck or a roast goose, filled with a rich stuffing, would call for a full-bodied red wine.

Meat

White wines like Graves or Rieslings go well with pork and veal — as do the lighter reds like Beaujolais or Zinfandel. A rosé might be nice with pork chops cooked with fruit. With veal Italian-style (like veal-and-peppers), you could try an Italian white (like Soave or a white Chianti) or a dry red like Bardolino. Veal in a cream sauce may be paired with one of the fuller-bodied white Burgundies or a light red Bordeaux. A simply baked ham is most often accompanied by a light red wine, though many prefer a white wine. Cold ham that has been prepared with something sweet takes well to a chilled rosé. Beef and lamb (particularly those marinated in red wine) are usually best accompanied by the fuller red wines. For Italian dishes, Chianti is the most frequent choice, though barolo and barbaresco are excellent. The finer the cut of meat, or the more elaborate the preparation, the better the wine should be. For example, an excellent Médoc would pay proper homage to a splendid filet of beef, whereas California Mountain Red would be perfectly adequate for hamburgers or pot roast. Casseroles and stews are, of course, served with wines that complement their main ingredients; for very informal meals, California's Zinfandel and Mountain Red are inexpensive but very agreeable choices for hearty meat stews and ragouts.

Game

Game birds (quail, pheasant, Rock Cornish hens, etc.) may be accompanied by a light red Burgundy or Bordeaux. A heavier wine will better complement the strong-flavored game like venison.

Variety Meats

Calf's liver and chicken liver are most often served with a light red wine — although if they are prepared in white wine and delicately seasoned, one of the fuller whites would be better. Sweetbreads are generally accompanied by light, dry white wines; brains with a somewhat fuller white. Beef liver and kidneys usually take best to the full-bodied reds.

Salads

Salads with vinegar dressings are better left unaccompanied by wine; not only will they tend to overpower the wine but may make *it* taste vinegary. If you are serving the salad *after* the main course and wish to continue with the wine you drank, that is up to you. And of course, if the salad is accompanying the main course, that does not mean you must refrain from serving any wine at all — just so long as it is not one of the finer ones. If you are serving a salad as the main course, and its dressing is not one where vinegar dominates (such as Prawn or Crab Louis, or perhaps a cold beef salad *Parisienne*), let the main ingredients dictate the wine selection.

Cheese

Cheese fondue is traditionally served with a dry white wine. Otherwise, red wine is considered to be the proper companion to cheeses because of their rather full flavor. The hard and semihard cheeses (e.g., Gruyère or Emmenthaler, Gouda, etc.) complement the light-bodied red wines, as do the soft fermented cheeses (Camembert, Brie, Bel Paese, etc.). If, however, you are serving a cheese course to drink the remains of a white wine from dinner, you would do best to select a light cheese such as the Italian Fontina, Norwegian Tilsit, California's Monterey Jack, Muenster. The blue-veined cheeses (Roquefort, Gorgonzola, Stilton, etc.) are, of course, quite intense in flavor and may tend to overwhelm a good wine. Nevertheless, they are frequently served with full-bodied reds like Châteauneuf-du-Pape or the Italian Barolo. If you are serving cheese with fresh fruit, port is a nice companion.

Note: In America, the salad and cheese are often served *together* following the main course. To connoisseurs, this is an outrage because of their refusal to drink wine with salad (see above) and, at the same time, their love for the glorious pairing of good cheese and good wine. Of course, cheese is often served with fresh fruit as dessert — in which case, wine is usually not served (except for a good sherry or port, in some instances); instead, coffee follows, with brandy or a liqueur.

Dessert

Champagne is the classic dessert wine. With light desserts such as fruit ices, sherbets, bombes, *brut* champagne is usually offered at a formal dinner. With a rich dessert, however, a brut champagne may taste thin, even sour; better to select one labeled extra-dry or even *demi-sec* (semisweet). With many desserts (cakes, fresh fruit, soufflés, etc.), the traditional choice is sweet white wine like a Sauternes. Also served are the sweeter sherries, Madeira, tawny or ruby port (a *vintage* port is best saved for even later — perhaps with walnuts, a ripe melon, or an exceptional cheese). For fruit and cheese as dessert, see *note* above.

Sherry

Rhine and Moselle

Champagne

All Purpose Glasses

Brandy and Liqueurs

The Crystal-Clear Wine Glass Guide

While the more somber wine expert will probably tell you that there is a different traditional glass for each wine, the modern trend is, fortunately, toward the all-purpose glass, and the emphasis is on the enjoyment of the wine itself. But of course, while wine *can* be sipped from even a paper cup, a juice glass, or coffee mug, it is interesting to note why the more traditional wine glasses are preferred:

- *plain, clear glass* to exhibit the wine's crystal clarity and its natural beautiful color.
- *stemmed*, because lifting a *stemless* glass not only conceals the lovely wine but because the warmth of the hand interferes with the proper serving temperature and with the aroma.
- *at least an 8-ounce capacity*, so that an average serving (4 ounces) takes up only half (or less) of the glass, leaving plenty of empty space above for capturing the bouquet (aroma, fragrance).
- *tulip-shaped*, because the slightly inward-sloping sides help concentrate the bouquet inside for more pleasurable sniffing.

If you are choosing only one wine glass, the perfect all-purpose glass is the 9-ounce tulip shape, in which you can serve white, red, or rosé wine, or champagne. If you wish to select two, have an 8-ounce glass for white wine, a 10-ounce glass for red. If you would like a good champagne glass, in addition, take note that the familiar "saucer-bowl" glass (which often doubles as a *sherbet dish*!) is out of favor. The narrow, tall, somewhat tulip-shaped champagne glass is considered ideal for the encouragement and display of the wine's sparkling bubbles.

There are, of course, variously designed glasses for apéritif and after-dinner wines, sherry glasses, traditional glasses for Rhine and Mosel wines, etc. But they certainly are not at all necessary for the enjoyment of good wine.

How to Use the Recipes

Herbs: For convenience and practicality (since relatively few people have ready access to fresh herbs), the measurements for herbs in these recipes refer to the commercial *dried* herbs (except for parsley, available at most supermarkets, and whenever an herb is to serve as a garnish). Where a sprig of thyme is suggested as a component of a *bouquet garni* but is not available, ¼ teaspoon dried thyme may be added to the pot in its place. If you *are* fortunate enough to have your own little herb garden, double the quantity specified in the recipe (dried herbs are considerably concentrated in flavor) — or add to taste.

Oven: Remember to *preheat* the oven so that it will have reached the specified temperature by the time you're ready to use.

Wine: Following each recipe is a notation — *the wine* — which lists a few suggestions for the appropriate wine to be used *in* and served *with* the dish.

Taste: No recipe, no matter how detailed, is ever a total substitute for your own taste buds. So do not hesitate to taste-test your dish as you go along (unless, of course, you're dealing with uncooked pork!), or at least before serving, and adjust the seasoning balance as necessary.

The old adage, "the better the wine, the better the dish," can be applied to *all* the ingredients used for a recipe. Even though we have stuck to measurements for dried herbs, fresh ones, if you can get them, are infinitely superior. So too with grinding pepper from a pepper mill instead of shaking it out of a supermarket shaker. Cheese, freshly grated, is exquisite. (I use the packaged versions of "grated" Parmesan and Romano, for example, in only the most dire circumstances.)

Canned broth and bouillon we have *all* come to rely on — even the most redoubtable of culinary experts — and they are indeed handy, especially when the amount required is small. But I would not think of preparing French Onion Soup, for instance, or the Belgian Waterzooie of Chicken with anything *but* my own homemade stock (which I keep frozen, in small one-use quantities, for just such purposes).

Grated lemon and orange peel from the fruits themselves are vastly superior to the dried ones found on spice shelves. So too with lemon juice, the bottled varieties of which are simply not as good as the juice from the beautiful lemon itself.

Four Keys to the Kingdom of Wine Cookery

1. Any wine that is not fit to drink is not fit to cook with. I refer *especially* to the so-called "cooking" wines sold in supermarkets — and to the inferior vineyard products as well. Their harsh, unpleasant flavor will concentrate during cooking and dominate the other ingredients — virtually ruining the taste of the dish. This does not mean however, that expensive vintage wines are essential (though you may *want* to use them in certain outstanding dishes for special occasions). For most purposes, the good but inexpensive wines available so readily throughout this country will prove more than adequate.

2. Always keep in mind that in cooking with wine, the alcohol (*and* its calories, it might be noted) evaporates, leaving only the inimitable flavor. This is important not only to teetotalers and waist-watchers but for those with discriminating palates — for the wine flavor is changed and intensified. Therefore, if you are adding wine at the *end* of cooking, let it boil up or simmer for a moment or two before removing from heat. Or boil it in a separate pan first,

until somewhat reduced. (If, during this latter process, the alcohol in the wine catches fire, don't panic. Just let the flames burn out — or clamp a lid over the pan — and continue cooking as before.)

3. A good rule to remember — and not only when cooking with wine — is that heavy-handedness is seldom a virtue. So if you are experimenting with a new wine-dish creation of your own, start out . . . yes, fearlessly *but* gradually. It goes without saying that you would no more pour in the whole bottle of wine automatically than you would, say, throw in a handful of dried oregano or chili powder.

4. Substituting another liquid for the wine called for in a recipe is usually ill-advised. If you do not have the wine specified, turn to a recipe that you are better prepared for at the moment. Of course, if a very small amount is required, you *can* substitute an appropriate liquid — be it broth or stock, fruit or tomato juice, water, whatever. But it would be quite senseless to make, let us say, *Coq au Vin* or Beef *Bourguignonne* solely with beef broth.

Substituting another *wine* for the one specified in a recipe is often a rather tricky business. But it can be done, provided you are familiar with the dish and the type of wine that should go in it. For example, dry white (French) vermouth is frequently a substitute for dry white wine. If you do not have a Sauternes on hand, try another sweet white wine. There may be instances when a sherry will pinch-hit for port or Marsala.

THE WINE CHEF'S HORS D'OEUVRES

Escargots a la Bourguignonne

½ pound sweet butter,
  softened
3 tablespoons minced shallots
3 cloves garlic, minced
¼ cup minced parsley

Salt and freshly ground
  black pepper, to taste
4 dozen prepared snails*
Dry white wine
Fresh breadcrumbs

Cream the butter with shallots, garlic, parsley, salt, and pepper until thoroughly blended. Place a little of this snail-butter in the bottom of each shell. Slip in the snail and fill generously with more of the butter mixture. Place in hollows of snail dishes, pour a tablespoon of wine over each one, and dust lightly with breadcrumbs. Bake in 400° oven until hot and melting — about 8 minutes. Serve at once, with French bread for "mopping up" the luscious butter sauce. Serves 8.

the wine: a white Burgundy (perhaps a Puligny-Montrachet), or a Graves, or one from the Loire, like Pouilly-Fumé. Or a California Pinot (either Blanc or Chardonnay). If you prefer a red wine, a Burgundy or Bordeaux.

*Prepared imported snails (with shells) are available in cans at gourmet-food shops and departments. Simply wash the snails and the shells according to label directions.

Special accoutrements for serving escargots — snail plates, little tongs used for holding the hot shell, and tiny forks for digging out the snail — are available but not necessary for the enjoyment of this dish. Simply use seafood forks and hold onto the shells with napkin-protected fingers.

Mussels a la Mariniere

4 dozen mussels
4 shallots, minced
4 sprigs parsley
2 sprigs thyme
1 bay leaf
1 rib celery, chopped

1 carrot, chopped
Freshly ground black pepper,
  to taste
¼ cup butter
1½ cups dry white wine
¼ cup chopped parsley

Under cold running water, scrub the mussels well with a wire brush or scrape with a knife. Remove "beards" with scissors. Discard all mussels with cracked or opened shells, and wash again.

Combine remaining ingredients (except chopped parsley) in a large kettle and simmer gently for 5 to 10 minutes. Add mussels, cover tightly, and steam until the shells have opened (shaking the pot occasionally) — about 5 to 10 minutes. Discard any mussels whose shells have not opened.

They may be served in their whole shells or, if you prefer, remove the top shells. Arrange in deep heated soup plates or large serving dish. Add chopped parsley to cooking liquid, reheat for a couple of minutes, and ladle over mussels. Serve at once, with hot buttered French bread. (The mussels may be eaten with the fingers or with seafood forks.) Serves 8.

the wine: a Riesling or Chablis.

Also a wonderful main course for an informal lunch or supper, served with French bread, as above, a green salad, and dessert. Serves 4.

Coquilles St. Jacques

1½ pounds scallops
1¼ cups dry white wine
4 shallots, minced

Pinch of white pepper
1 cup cream

1 tablespoon flour
2 tablespoons butter, softened
¼ cup fresh-grated cheese
   (Swiss or Gruyère)
½ cup fresh breadcrumbs
2 tablespoons melted butter

Wash scallops well in cold water, and dry. (If using the tiny bay scallops, leave whole; if they're the larger sea scallops, cut in quarters.) Combine scallops in saucepan with wine, shallots, salt, and pepper. Bring to a boil, then cover and simmer over low heat just until tender — about 3 to 5 minutes. Remove scallops with slotted spoon and divide among six coquilles* or individual heatproof rame-kins. Cook the liquid in saucepan over high heat until reduced by half. Lower heat, stir in the cream, and cook until sauce is reduced and slightly thickened, stirring often; *do not boil.* Knead together the flour and 2 tablespoons butter. Lower heat and gradually drop in the flour-butter mixture *(beurre manié)*, bit by bit; stir and cook until well blended. Pour sauce over the scallops, and sprinkle with grated cheese. Combine breadcrumbs with melted butter and scatter over top. Slip under broiler just until tops are delicately browned. Serves 6.

the wine: a white Burgundy or Graves. Or, from California, Dry Sé-millon or Dry Sauvignon Blanc.

*Coquilles (shells in which food is cooked and served) are sold in culinary shops and departments.

Swiss Cheese Fondue

1 clove garlic
2 cups dry white wine
A few drops of lemon juice
½ pound each Emmenthaler and
    Gruyère cheese, freshly grated
3 tablespoons flour
3 tablespoons kirsch*

Salt
Freshly ground black pepper
Freshly grated nutmeg
   1 tablespoon butter
A large loaf of crusty French or
    Italian bread, cut into 1-inch
    chunks

Peel garlic and rub it over the inside of your fondue pot or heavy flameproof chafing dish. Pour in wine, add lemon juice, and bring just to the boiling point over a moderate flame. Combine the cheese with the flour and gradually add it to the pot, stirring constantly with fork or wooden spoon until cheese has melted and you have a thick creamy mixture. Add kirsch, season lightly with salt, pepper, and nutmeg, and stir in the butter. Transfer pot to fondue warmer or, if using a chafing dish, set it over hot water; the fondue should be simmering very gently, not boiling.

Each guest will spear a cube of bread with a long-handled fork (use the

*a colorless cherry brandy made in France and Germany.

44

special fondue forks if you have them), dip it into the cheese mixture and swirl it around. At the end is the *pièce de resistance:* a delicious crust of cheese on the bottom of the pot, to be scraped off and savored. Serves 4 to 6.

      the wine: the Swiss Neuchâtel is perfect for this dish, both *in* the fondue and to serve with it. A Chablis or Riesling would also be good.

Of course, cheese fondue is frequently served as the main event — especially nice for a late supper. Follow with a luscious dessert of fresh fruits — and coffee.

Quiche Lorraine

½ cup finely chopped shallots
   (or mild onions)
½ cup dry white wine
 8 strips thick-sliced bacon
 6 eggs
 3 cups heavy cream

¼ teaspoon salt
Pinch each of white pepper and
   grated nutmeg
¾ pound Swiss cheese (Gruyère
   or Emmenthaler), grated
 1 tablespoon butter
 1 large pastry shell*

Combine shallots (or onions) and wine in small saucepan; bring to a boil, lower heat, and simmer for a couple of minutes. Remove from heat and let cool.

Cut bacon into ¼-inch pieces; brown lightly in frying pan, drain well on paper towels, and scatter over bottom of pastry shell.

Beat together the eggs and cream, just enough to blend. Add salt, pepper, nutmeg, and shallot-wine mixture. Sprinkle grated cheese over the bacon. Pour in the egg mixture, and distribute bits of butter on top. Bake at 375° until puffed and golden-brown — about 30 minutes. Serves 8 to 10.

the wine: an Alsatian wine like Traminer (also produced in California).

Quiche Lorraine also makes a lovely main course for a luncheon or light supper — in which case, this recipe will serve 5 or 6. All you need is a green salad — and fruit for dessert.

*Prepare a 10-inch flan or pie shell (it should be about 2 inches high) from your favorite recipe or mix. Prebake just until it starts to take on color, according to directions for baking an unfilled shell.

Mushrooms a la Grecque

6 tablespoons olive oil
1 large onion, diced
1 carrot diced
¾ cup dry white wine
1 tablespoon lemon juice
Salt, to taste
6 coriander seeds

6 whole peppercorns
1 clove garlic
Bouquet garni*
1 pound small mushroom caps
1 large ripe tomato, peeled, seeded, cut into wedges
1 teaspoon sugar

garnish: *chopped parsley*

Heat 4 tablespoons of the olive oil in large heavy skillet. Add onion and carrot, and sauté until soft. Add wine, lemon juice, salt, coriander seeds, peppercorns, garlic, and *bouquet garni*. Bring to a boil. Add mushroom caps, tomato wedges, and dust with sugar. Cook, uncovered, over moderate heat for about 15 minutes. Remove from heat and let cool. Remove garlic and *bouquet garni*, and add remaining olive oil. Serve chilled, garnished with a sprinkling of chopped parsley. Serves 4 to 6.

Bouquet garni: 2 sprigs parsley, 1 sprig thyme, 1 bay leaf, and 1 rib of celery, tied together.

Mushrooms in Madeira Cream

1¼ pounds small fresh mushrooms
3 tablespoons butter
1 tablespoon oil
2 shallots, minced (or 2 scallions, white part only)
1 tablespoon flour
¾ cup medium cream
¼ cup dry Madeira

Salt and white pepper, to taste
Lemon juice
Pinch of grated nutmeg (optional)

serve over: *slices of hot buttered toast*

garnish: *chopped parsley*

Wash the mushrooms; remove stems and reserve for another use. Heat the butter and oil in a heavy saucepan or skillet, and sauté the mushroom caps until they are golden — about 6 minutes. Add minced shallots (or scallions) and cook for another minute or so. Lower heat, blend in the flour, and cook and stir for a couple of minutes. Stir in the cream and Madeira, and cook over low heat for about 15 minutes, stirring often. Remove from heat and season to taste with salt, pepper, lemon juice, and nutmeg. Spoon over hot buttered toast, and sprinkle with chopped parsley. Serve at once, while still hot. Serves 4 or 5.

Onions Monegasque

2 carrots, coarsely chopped
¼ cup olive oil
2 pounds tiny white onions (of
   uniform size, if possible)
2 cups water
½ cup dry white wine
¼ cup lemon juice
1 tablespoon tomato paste
1 bay leaf

½ teaspoon thyme
Sprig of fennel (optional)
1 teaspoon sugar
Salt and freshly ground black
   pepper, to taste
1 cup golden seedless raisins

garnish: *finely chopped parsley*

Sauté chopped carrots in hot olive oil until soft and golden. Peel onions and place in a saucepan, along with the water, wine, and lemon juice. Stir in the tomato paste; then add the sautéed carrots, bay leaf, thyme, fennel (if using), sugar, salt, and pepper. Simmer until the onions are just tender. Add raisins and cook until sauce has reduced a little. Cool, then chill.

Before serving, correct seasoning if necessary, drizzle with a little olive oil if you like, and sprinkle with chopped parsley. Serves 8.

Oeufs en Gelee

1 envelope (1 tablespoon)
   unflavored gelatin
2 cups clear beef or chicken
   consommé (homemade or
   canned)
3 tablespoons port
4 fresh tarragon leaves
   (optional)

4 ovals or rounds of cooked ham
4 poached or coddled eggs,
   drained and chilled
garnish: sprigs of watercress or
   parsley, or chopped aspic

Sprinkle gelatin over consommé in a saucepan, and let stand for several minutes to soften. Stir over low heat until gelatin is completely dissolved. Remove from heat and stir in the port.

Pour a thin layer (about ⅛-inch) of cold liquid aspic into 4 oval eggs-in-aspic molds (or custard cups), and chill until set. If tarragon leaves are available, dip them into cold liquid aspic and place atop the set jelly. Do the same with ham slices. Place a poached or coddled egg in each mold atop the ham, and fill with cold liquid aspic. Chill until set — at least one hour.

Unmold, and garnish with parsley sprigs or watercress . . . though I prefer to garnish this dish with a border of chopped aspic: make another batch of aspic as above; chill it in a thin layer (about ¼-inch) in a plate or pan until set, then chop up just before serving and arrange around each mold. Serves 4.

Beefsteak Tartare

2 pounds lean beefsteak,
  twice-ground*
Salt, to taste
½ teaspoon dry English mustard
Worcestershire sauce
½ cup dry red wine
  1 tablespoon brandy

6 egg yolks
Capers, drained
Finely chopped onion
Finely chopped parsley
Black caviar
Black-pepper mill

Mix the ground beef with salt, dry mustard, a few dashes of Worcestershire, the wine, and brandy. Shape into 6 thick patties. Make a depression in the center of each patty and drop in an egg yolk. Arrange a circle of capers around the egg yolk, then a circle of chopped onion, then one of chopped parsley; finish with a border of black caviar. Grind black pepper over all. (Each guest will mix egg yolk and garnishes into meat.) Serve with toast or thin slices of good pumpernickel, rye, or French bread. Serves 6.

If this dish is to be served as part of a cocktail-party buffet, as it frequently is, dry sherry and chilled champagne are usually offered in addition to the standard drinks.

*Select a good lean cut of steak — such as fillet, top sirloin, or round steak — and put it through the grinder twice. Since you are serving raw beef, you must, of course, select meat of the highest quality. If it is impracticable for you to grind it, have the butcher do it. But make sure you are dealing with an absolutely reputable one (you wouldn't want him, for example, to put the meat through the same grinder he uses for pork!). And remember that Beefsteak Tartare must be very fresh.

THE WINE CHEF'S SOUPS

Cold Blueberry Soup

1 pint blueberries
Juice of 1 lemon
1 stick of cinnamon
1 quart of water
½ cup sugar (or to taste)
2 tablespoons cornstarch

¼ cup sherry or port
½ cup heavy cream

garnish: *whipped cream, a few
fresh blueberries, grated lemon
peel*

Pick over and wash the blueberries. Place in large saucepan; add lemon juice, cinnamon stick, and water. Bring to a boil, then cover and simmer until blueberries are somewhat mushy — about 10 to 15 minutes. Stir in the sugar. Mix the cornstarch to a paste with ¼ cup of water and stir into the hot berries. Bring again to a boil, then cook and stir for a couple of minutes. Remove from heat and discard cinnamon stick. Put the soup through a sieve or puree it in a blender. Stir in the sherry or port, let cool, then refrigerate until chilled.

Stir in the heavy cream just before serving. If desired, garnish each serving with a dollop of whipped cream, a few fresh berries, and a dusting of grated lemon peel. Serves 6 to 8.

This unusual and delightful summer appetizer soup is also served as a dessert in Scandinavia.

Bouillabaisse

½ cup olive oil
2 large onions, sliced
2 carrots, sliced
2 leeks, sliced
4 cloves garlic, crushed
4 ripe tomatoes, seeded and diced
2 quarts water
2 cups dry white wine
1 bay leaf
½ teaspoon thyme
¼ teaspoon powdered saffron
⅛ teaspoon fennel seed
1 teaspoon dried grated orange peel (packaged)

2 to 3 pounds fish trimmings (heads and bones)
Salt and freshly ground pepper
4 pounds assorted fish,* cleaned
1 dozen each cherrystone or littleneck clams and mussels
1 pound scallops
6 to 8 thick slices of French bread, brushed with garlic butter and toasted in oven

garnish: chopped parsley
serve with: rouille** (optional)

Heat olive oil in a large, heavy kettle or casserole. Add onions, carrots, leeks, and garlic; sauté until soft and golden. Add tomatoes and cook for another 5 minutes or so. Add water, wine, seasonings, and the fish trimmings. Bring to a

*such as cod, haddock, sea bass, flounder, halibut.
**Rouille is a very hot sauce and a frequent accompaniment to bouillabaisse and other Mediterranean fish soups. Simply blend dried hot red pepper flakes, according to taste, into mayonnaise (preferably homemade). Just one teaspoon floated atop a serving of soup is a real eye-opener!

boil, skim, and continue cooking at a slow boil, uncovered, for about 40 minutes. Strain, taste for seasoning, and add salt and pepper to taste. (If not using immediately, let cool, then refrigerate.)

Cut the fish into 2-inch pieces. Scrub the clams well under cold running water. Scrub the mussels well under running water, wash them thoroughly, and remove "beards" with scissors. Wash the scallops too, of course.

Bring soup to a boil. Add fish and cook, uncovered, for 15 minutes, stirring gently from time to time. Add clams, mussels, and scallops, and continue cooking just until the shells open. Gently lift out the seafood, arrange on a hot serving platter, and spoon a little soup over. Taste soup for seasoning. Place the toasted garlic-bread slices in tureen or large serving bowl and pour in the hot soup. Sprinkle with a handful of chopped parsley. Serve at once, accompanied by *rouille* if desired. Each guest will help himself to the soup and the seafood; provide forks as well as soup spoons, and additional hot French bread. Serves 6 to 8.

the wine: any of the three types may be enjoyed with bouillabaisse: white (a Burgundy or Rhône, or Pouilly-Fumé, or a Riesling); red (like Beaujolais or Beaune, or California Mountain Red or Zinfandel); or a rosé.

Bouillabaisse makes a hearty and magnificent meal on a cold winter's day or night! All you need is a loaf of hot French bread. If you like, follow with a simple green salad and a good cheese. If there's room for dessert, try sliced sugared oranges doused with Grand Marnier.

Cream of Artichoke

3 tablespoons butter
2 tablespoons flour
1 small onion, chopped
1 rib celery, chopped
1 small leek, chopped
2 sprigs parsley, finely chopped
4 cups chicken stock
½ cup dry white wine

1 package (10 ounces) frozen
    artichoke hearts, thawed
Salt and freshly ground black
    pepper to taste
½ cup light cream
¼ cup dry sherry

garnish: *finely chopped chervil or
parsley. Or snipped chives.*

Melt butter in a large, heavy saucepan; stir in the flour and cook until completely smooth, stirring constantly. Add onion, celery, leek, parsley, chicken stock, and wine, and simmer for about 15 to 20 minutes. Strain. Add artichoke hearts and cook until they are tender. Puree the soup in a blender or put it through a fine sieve. Season to taste with salt and pepper. If serving hot, return to saucepan and bring back to boil. If serving chilled, let cool, then refrigerate. In either case, stir in the cream and sherry just before serving. Garnish, if desired. Serves 4 to 6.

Gazpacho

4 large, very ripe tomatoes
1 clove garlic
1 small onion
1 small green pepper
1 small cucumber
½ cup olive oil
½ cup dry red wine

Salt, to taste
½ teaspoon ground cumin
2 cups tomato juice
Block of ice
garnishes: *chopped tomatoes,
onion, cucumber, green pepper.
And croutons.*

Cut up the tomatoes and place in blender along with the garlic; blend at high speed for a few seconds. Cut up the onion, green pepper, and cucumber; add to tomatoes and blend again. Strain into a tureen or large serving bowl and refrigerate until well chilled. Freeze a block of ice in a small metal or plastic bowl.

Just before serving, mix together the olive oil, wine, salt, cumin, and tomato juice, and stir into the chilled tomato mixture. Add block of ice. Set out small bowls of the chopped garnishes and croutons, to which your guests will help themselves. (I prefer homemade croutons, by the way, made simply by frying diced bread in butter until crisp and golden.) Serves 4 to 6.

Although frequently enjoyed as an appetizer, gazpacho can also serve as a lovely main course at a summer luncheon. If you like, start out with a dry sherry and light hors d'oeuvre — perhaps green Spanish olives, toasted almonds, and slices of sausage (like chorizo *or the Italian* peperone). *With the soup, you might wish to serve a homemade herb bread. End with a fruit dessert: poached peaches or pears, for example, with a custard sauce.*

Waterzooie of Chicken

1 chicken (about 4 to 5 pounds), cut up
⅓ cup butter
3 carrots
3 ribs celery
2 leeks
1 parsnip (optional)
1 small onion, quartered
Salt and white pepper
3 sprigs parsley
½ bay leaf

¼ teaspoon fines herbes, *thyme or tarragon*
2 cloves
⅛ teaspoon grated nutmeg
1 cup dry white wine or dry white (French) vermouth
Clear chicken broth*
1 lemon, thinly sliced
2 tablespoons finely chopped parsley
6 egg yolks
½ cup heavy cream

   Rub the chicken pieces with butter (softened) and brown on all sides under broiler — or melt butter in heavy skillet and brown chicken in it. Cut carrots, celery, leeks, and parsnip (if using) into julienne sticks. Arrange chicken pieces in casserole, and top with the vegetables, including the quartered onion. Season to taste with salt and pepper; add parsley, bay leaf, your choice of herb, the

*If using canned broth, chill the cans before using; then simply skim off the fat that has risen to the surface.

cloves, and nutmeg. Pour in the wine, then just enough chicken broth to almost cover the chicken. Bring to a boil, then cover, and simmer slowly over low heat or in a 325° oven until chicken is done — about 30 minutes. Skim off fat and taste for seasoning.

Add lemon slices and chopped parsley to casserole. Beat together the egg yolks and cream with a wire whisk. Slowly drizzle a little of the hot soup into egg-yolk mixture, beating constantly. Pour into casserole and slowly swirl the casserole over medium heat until sauce thickens slightly; do not let boil. Serve from the casserole, in large soup plates. (Your diners will need knives and forks as well as soup spoons for this dish.) Serves 4 to 6.

the wine: a white Burgundy or Bordeaux (a dry Graves). Or, from California, Dry Sauvignon Blanc or Dry Sémillon.

Call it soup or stew, this Flemish creation is a superb contribution to the joys and the art of chicken cookery. Although it is often served in Belgium as one of many courses, Waterzooie will proudly serve as a meal in its own right. Traditionally served with boiled potatoes, but you may also want to add a loaf of cracked wheat bread or good French bread, along with a crock of sweet butter. If you would like to start off with a first course, try the Belgians' much-loved Tomates aux Crevettes: tiny shrimps mixed with mayonnaise (preferably home-made) and stuffed into fat, juicy-ripe tomatoes.

French Onion Soup Gratinee

½ cup butter
1 tablespoon olive oil
1 to 1½ pounds onions (preferably
   yellow), thinly sliced
1 teaspoon sugar
1 tablespoon flour
2 quarts beef bouillon
1 cup dry red wine

1 small bay leaf
¼ teaspoon thyme
Salt and freshly ground black
   pepper
A loaf of French bread
Melted butter or olive oil
½ pound Swiss cheese (preferably
   Gruyère), grated
¼ cup cognac

Heat butter and oil in a large heavy pot. Add onions, dust with sugar, and cook and stir until they are soft and golden. Sprinkle flour over the onions; stir to blend it in, taking care that it does not burn. Gradually stir in the beef bouillon until it begins to boil. Add wine, bay leaf, and thyme. Lower heat, cover, and simmer very gently for 30 to 45 minutes. Season to taste with salt and pepper.

Cut the bread into slices about 1-inch thick and brush lightly on both sides with melted butter or oil. Arrange on a baking sheet and place in 325° oven until lightly toasted, turning once.

In the bottom of a large, heavy casserole or ovenproof tureen, arrange three layers of the toasted bread slices, sprinkling about ½ cup grated cheese over each layer. Add cognac to the hot soup and pour it into the casserole. Cover with remaining grated cheese and place in a 450° oven until cheese is golden and bubbling. Serves 4 to 6.

the wine: a red Burgundy or Bordeaux, or a red Rhône wine like Châteauneuf-du-Pape. From California, Pinot Noir or Cabernet Sauvignon.

Although this soup is often served as a preliminary course, I like to make a full meal of it — especially on a cold winter's day! Salad and a bottle of wine are all you'll need with it.

San Francisco Cioppino

2½ pounds fish (striped bass and halibut), cut in pieces

1½ pounds fresh shrimp

2 dozen each mussels and littleneck clams

1 large fresh or frozen Dungeness crab (or a 1½-pound lobster, cut up)

4 tablespoons olive oil

1 tablespoon butter

2 large onions, chopped

1 large green pepper, seeded and chopped

2 ribs celery, sliced

A few fresh mushrooms, sliced

3 cloves garlic, minced

1 can (about 2 pounds) tomatoes

1 1-pound can tomato sauce

2 cups dry red wine

1 bay leaf

¼ teaspoon each oregano and basil

2 cloves

Thin strip of lemon peel

½ cup finely chopped parsley

Salt and freshly ground black pepper, to taste

garnish: chopped parsley

Prepare the seafood for cooking: wash the fish; shell and clean the shrimp; scrub the mussels well under running water and remove "beards" with scissors; scrub the clams; crack and clean the crab.

Heat oil and butter in a large heavy skillet. Add onions, green pepper, celery, mushrooms, and garlic; sauté until soft, stirring often. Pour in the tomatoes, tomato sauce, and wine, and add remaining ingredients. Bring to a boil, then cover, lower heat, and simmer for 15 to 20 minutes, stirring occasionally.

Place the fish, shrimp, and crab in a large deep casserole. Pour soup over, cover, and cook over low heat — or in a 300° oven — for 30 minutes. Add mussels and clams and cook just until the shells open — about 7 to 10 minutes. If desired, garnish with chopped parsley. Serve in large heated soup plates, with plenty of hot crusty Italian bread. Serves 6 to 8.

the wine: an Italian red, like Chianti or Valpolicella.

This soup makes a meal in itself. Add a green salad along with the bread. For dessert, cheese, fresh fruit — and espresso.

Creole Gumbo

¼ cup butter
2 tablespoons oil
1 large onion, chopped
1 green pepper, chopped
3 tablespoons flour
Bouquet garni*
1 clove garlic, minced
1 thin strip lemon peel
½ teaspoon Worcestershire
Tabasco
Salt and freshly ground black
    pepper, to taste

1 pound crabmeat (fresh, frozen,
    or canned), flaked
2 dozen small shrimp, shelled,
    cleaned, cooked
1 large can (about 2 pounds)
    tomatoes
1 can (8 ounces) okra
1½ cups milk
½ cup light cream
¼ cup dry sherry

garnish: chopped parsley

Heat together the butter and oil in a large heavy saucepan. Add onion and green pepper, and sauté until soft. Blend in the flour; cook and stir until smooth and thickened. Add *bouquet garni*, garlic, lemon peel, Worcestershire, a drop or two of Tabasco, and salt and pepper. Add the crabmeat and shrimp, then empty

*Bouquet garni: 2 sprigs parsley, 1 sprig thyme, 1 bay leaf, and 1 rib of celery, tied together.

the canned tomatoes and okra (both undrained) into the pot. Bring to a boil; lower heat, cover, and simmer for about 20 to 25 minutes. Gradually stir in the milk and cream; cook and stir just until heated through. Add sherry, discard *bouquet garni*, and sprinkle with a little chopped parsley. Serves 4 to 6.

the wine: a domestic Dry Sauvignon Blanc, Chenin Blanc, or Grey Riesling.

If you wish to make this gumbo the focal point of your meal — especially nice for a winter luncheon — you need add only a tossed green salad and hot French bread or Southern biscuits. For dessert, perhaps an old-fashioned Ambrosia, with rum pecan cookies.

THE WINE CHEF'S MAIN DISHES

Chicken Dijonnaise

2 large chicken breasts, split
Salt and freshly ground pepper
¼ cup butter
1 small onion, finely chopped
¼ cup dry white wine
¼ cup chicken broth
2 tablespoons orange juice

2 teaspoons flour
1 teaspoon Dijon-style mustard
2 tablespoons heavy cream
1 teaspoon grated orange peel

garnish: *sprigs of watercress or parsley*

Remove skin and bones from split chicken breasts (or have your butcher do it). Sprinkle with salt and pepper. Heat butter in a heavy skillet, add chicken, and cook quickly until browned on both sides. Add onions and sauté until soft and golden. Add wine, chicken broth, orange juice. Cover and simmer gently until chicken is tender — about 15 to 20 minutes. Remove chicken to heated serving platter. Stir flour into skillet and heat to the boiling point, stirring constantly; simmer for a minute or two. Strain through a fine sieve. Stir in mustard, heavy cream, and grated orange peel; taste for seasoning. Reheat gently if necessary, but do not let boil. Pour sauce over chicken, and garnish. Serves 4.

the wine: a white Burgundy. Or Pinot Blanc from California.

serve with: parsley rice or boiled new potatoes. The vegetable might be tiny green peas (petits pois) or asparagus.

Beef Bourguignonne

¼ pound piece of salt pork or lean
    bacon, diced
¼ cup butter
  2 tablespoons olive oil
  3 pounds boneless beef (top or
    bottom round, or rump), cut in
    2-inch cubes
Flour
Salt and freshly ground black
    pepper, to taste
¼ cup cognac
  1 cup diced onions
  2 carrots, diced
1 or 2 cloves garlic, minced

  1 tablespoon tomato paste
Bouquet garni*
  3 cups red Burgundy
  1 cup beef stock (or water)
12 to 18 tiny white onions
½ teaspoon sugar
12 to 18 mushroom caps
Small wedge of lemon
More butter

garnish: chopped parsley

Put salt pork or bacon in saucepan with cold water to cover; simmer for 5 to 10 minutes. Rinse in cold water, drain, and dry on paper towels.

Heat 3 tablespoons butter and the oil in large heavy skillet. Brown the diced salt pork or bacon until crisp, then remove with slotted spoon to a large casserole. Coat the beef cubes in flour and brown on all sides in the same skillet. Season with

*Bouquet garni: 1 rib of celery, 1 bay leaf, 1 sprig thyme, and 2 or 3 sprigs of parsley, tied together.

salt and pepper. Warm the cognac, pour over the meat, and set aflame. (Have a lid at hand to clamp over the pot in case the flames rise too high.) When flame has died out, transfer meat to casserole. Add onions, carrots, and garlic to the skillet and sauté until soft and golden, stirring often. Stir in tomato paste, and transfer contents of the skillet to casserole. Add the *bouquet garni*, pour in the wine, and add beef stock or water to just cover the meat. Bring to the boiling point atop stove. Then cover tightly and place in a 325° oven (or over a very low flame) until meat is tender — about 2½ hours.

Melt about 1 tablespoon butter in a skillet or saucepan; add onions, dust with sugar, and sauté until lightly browned; transfer to casserole and continue cooking for another half-hour. Melt another tablespoon or so of butter; add mushroom caps, squeeze the lemon wedge over them; and sauté for about 5 minutes. Add to casserole and cook for 10 to 15 minutes more. Skim off fat, discard *bouquet garni*, taste for seasoning, and sprinkle with chopped parsley. Serves 6.

the wine: a red Burgundy, like a Nuits St.-Georges or a Pommard. Or, from California, Pinot Noir. California's Mountain Red would also be suitable.

serve with: a loaf of hot, crusty French bread and a crisp green salad. Follow with fresh fruit and cheese. Beef Bourguignonne is occasionally accompanied by noodles, rice or boiled potatoes and preceded by a clear soup or a cold seafood hors d'oeuvre.

Navarin of Lamb

3 pounds boneless shoulder of
    lamb
½ cup butter
2 tablespoons lard or cooking oil
1 large onion, sliced
3 tablespoons flour
1 teaspoon sugar
Salt and freshly ground black
    pepper
2 cloves garlic, minced
Bouquet garni*
2 cups dry red wine
½ cup beef bouillon (or water)

½ cup tomato puree
1 teaspoon Kitchen Bouquet
    (optional)
18 tiny white onions
12 tiny new potatoes, peeled and
    halved
6 small turnips, peeled and halved
6 small carrots, scraped and
    halved
Optional: 1 package frozen (whole
    or cut) green beans, partially
    thawed

garnish: *chopped parsley*

Have excess fat trimmed from lamb; lamb should be cut into 2-inch cubes. In a large heavy casserole or Dutch oven, heat half the butter with the lard or oil. Add lamb and sliced onion, and brown the lamb on all sides. Blend in the flour,

*Bouquet garni: 4 sprigs parsley, 1 bay leaf, a sprig of thyme, tied together.

and stir over low heat until thickened and the flour is brown. Sprinkle with ¾ teaspoon sugar, toss over heat for a few moments, and season to taste with salt and pepper. Add garlic, *bouquet garni*, then stir in the wine, beef bouillon or water, tomato puree, and Kitchen Bouquet (if using). Cover and place in a 350° oven (or simmer gently over low heat) for 1 hour.

Pour the casserole into a colander (set over a pot). Discard *bouquet garni*. Pick out whatever bits of skin or bone there might be from the lamb. Rinse out the casserole or use another one. Skim off fat from surface of sauce, and taste for seasoning. Return lamb to clean casserole and pour sauce over it.

Melt remaining butter in a large heavy skillet. Add onions, potatoes, turnips, and carrots. Dust with remaining sugar, and sauté until lightly browned. Add to the casserole, and baste with sauce. Bring to a boil atop stove, then cover and return to oven until meat and vegetables are tender — about 30 minutes. If desired, add package of green beans during the last 5 minutes of cooking. Garnish with a sprinkling of chopped parsley. Serves 6.

> *the wine:* a red Burgundy or Bordeaux (like a Pomerol). Or from California, Pinot Noir or Zinfandel.

> *serve with:* a crisp green salad and, if you like, hot French bread. Follow with fresh fruit and cheese.

Osso Buco

4 meaty veal shanks, sawed into
    pieces about 2 inches long
Flour
Salt and freshly ground black
    pepper
¼ cup butter
2 tablespoons olive oil
1 medium onion, finely chopped
1 carrot, finely chopped
1 leek, finely chopped
2 ribs celery, finely chopped
2 cloves garlic, minced

1 cup dry white wine or dry
    white (French) vermouth
½ cup tomato puree
1 cup veal stock (or chicken or
    beef broth)
Bouquet garni*
½ teaspoon basil
Gremolata:
Grated peel of 1 orange
Grated peel of 1 lemon
1 clove garlic, minced
1 anchovy fillet, minced
    (optional)

Dredge the veal shanks in flour, then season them with salt and pepper. If possible, select a heavy casserole that is large enough to hold the meat in one layer. In it, heat the butter and oil, and brown the meat. Add remaining ingredients (except the *gremolata*), cover, and simmer gently over low heat or bake in a

*Bouquet garni: 4 sprigs of parsley and 1 bay leaf, tied together.

325° oven until tender — about 1½ hours. Taste for seasoning and discard *bouquet garni*. Tip casserole and skim off fat. Mix together the ingredients for the *gremolata* and sprinkle evenly over the meat. Serve from casserole. Serves 4.

the wine: Chianti

serve with: saffron rice (especially Risotto alla Milanese) and a green salad. If you like, follow with a selection of Italian cheeses, served with Italian bread and butter and more wine.

The traditional grand finale of this Italian classic is the savoring of the marrow inside the bone.

Coq au Vin

1 3-pound chicken, cut up
¼ pound piece of lean bacon
¼ cup butter
2 tablespoons olive oil
12 tiny white onions
12 small mushroom caps
Flour
Salt and freshly ground black
    pepper
¼ cup cognac
3 cups dry red wine

1 cup beef broth
2 cloves garlic, minced
1 bay leaf
Pinch of thyme
2 sprigs parsley
1 tablespoon tomato puree
Pinch of sugar
2 tablespoons flour
2 tablespoons butter

garnish: *chopped parsley*

    Place the bacon in a small saucepan with cold water to cover. Let simmer for 5 to 10 minutes, then rinse in cold water, drain, and dry. Cut into dice.

    In a heavy casserole or Dutch oven, heat the butter and oil; add cubes of bacon and sauté until golden. Add onions, and sauté for another couple of minutes; then add mushrooms and continue cooking until they just start to brown. Remove with slotted spoon.

Roll chicken pieces in flour, place in casserole, and cook until golden brown on all sides. Pour in cognac and set aflame. Let burn for a few moments, shaking the pot until flames subside. Pour in the wine and beef broth; add garlic, bay leaf, thyme, and parsley, onions, mushrooms, and bacon bits. Stir in tomato puree, add sugar, and season with salt and pepper, to taste. Cover and simmer very gently (or bake in a 375° oven) until chicken is tender — about 30 to 40 minutes.

Drain casserole liquid into a saucepan and skim off fat. If necessary, boil down the liquid to reduce it to about 2 cups. Knead together the flour and butter; add it, bit by bit, to the liquid, beating constantly with a wire whisk until smooth. Taste for seasoning. Strain the sauce back into casserole. Cover and simmer gently (or place in a low oven) until chicken is heated through. Garnish, if desired, with chopped parsley. Serves 4.

the wine: a Beaujolais. Or, from California, Gamay Beaujolais.

serve with: boiled new potatoes in parsley-butter. Add green beans *amandine* and/or a green salad — and hot French bread.

Lasagne alla Bolognese

¼ cup butter
1 tablespoon olive oil
¼ pound lean bacon, finely chopped
1 large onion, finely chopped
1 rib of celery, finely chopped
1 large carrot, chopped
¼ pound mushrooms, chopped
2 pounds ground lean beef
1 can (about 2 pounds) Italian tomatoes
1 can (about 5 ounces) Italian tomato paste
¾ cup dry white wine
A thin strip of lemon peel

1 bay leaf
2 teaspoons Italian seasoning (mixed herbs) or 1 teaspoon each basil and oregano
2 cloves
1 teaspoon brown sugar
A few gratings of nutmeg
Salt and freshly ground black pepper, to taste
1-pound box of lasagna (preferably green)
3 cups hot Cream Sauce (see recipe for Lobster Thermidor)
¼ pound Parmesan cheese, grated
Butter

To make the Meat Sauce: Heat ¼ cup butter and olive oil in a large heavy frying pan. Add bacon, onion, celery, carrot and mushrooms. Sauté until bacon and onion are lightly browned — about 10 minutes — stirring often. Add ground beef; cook and stir until it is brown and crumbly. Add tomatoes, tomato paste, wine, lemon peel, bay leaf, herbs, cloves, brown sugar, nutmeg; season with salt and pepper. Cover and simmer gently for half an hour, stirring occasionally. Discard lemon peel and bay leaf; continue simmering, uncovered, until sauce has thickened somewhat — at least another half-hour.

Cook lasagne until *al dente* according to package directions. Drain carefully.

In a buttered rectangular baking dish (about 9-inch by 13-inch), make a layer of lasagne, overlapping them slightly. Top with some of the Meat Sauce, then with a thin layer of Cream Sauce, and sprinkle with a little grated Parmesan cheese. Repeat until all ingredients are used up, ending with Cream Sauce on top; sprinkle with remaining grated cheese and dot with butter. Bake at 350° until hot and bubbly and the top is lightly browned. Serves 6.

the wine: Chianti

serve with: crusty Italian bread and a tossed green salad. Start out with an antipasto platter (including, perhaps, capocollo or prosciutto, peperoncini; celery hearts and olives, marinated artichoke hearts or mushrooms, radishes, hard-cooked eggs) and breadsticks. In Italian homes and restaurants, antipasto is frequently accompanied by dry sherry or slightly chilled vermouth with a twist of lemon peel. For dessert, a *macedonia* of fresh fruit in brandy or Marsala, served with macaroons or anise cookies, and espresso.

Steak au Poivre

2 tablespoons peppercorns
  Tender sirloin or porterhouse
  steak (about 1½ inches thick)
1 tablespoon butter
2 teaspoons olive oil
2 shallots, minced (optional)

⅔ cup dry white wine or dry
  white vermouth
1 tablespoon cognac or brandy
2 tablespoons butter
garnish: watercress (optional)

Crush peppercorns coarsely, using a mortar and pestle or a rolling pin. Sprinkle half the pepper over one side of the steak, then press it into the meat with the heel of your hand. Repeat on other side. Let stand for about an hour, to allow flavor to penetrate the meat.

Heat butter and oil in a heavy skillet. Sear steak on both sides over high heat. Sauté to desired doneness (a 1½-inch steak should take about 4 or 5 minutes on each side for medium-rare). Remove steak to hot serving platter.

Add shallots to skillet (if using); stir in the wine and cognac or brandy. Simmer vigorously for a couple of minutes, scraping up sauté juices at bottom of pan with a wooden spoon. Remove from heat, swirl in the butter, and pour over steak. If desired, garnish with watercress. Serves 4.

the wine: a red Burgundy or Bordeaux. Or California's Pinot Noir or Cabernet Sauvignon.

serve with: very crisp French-fried or home-fried potatoes. Or baked potatoes. Add whole green beans, if you like, and French bread. Thick slices of beefsteak tomatoes with rings of Spanish onion, drizzled with oil and vinegar, make an ideal accompaniment.

Whole Salmon au Court Bouillon

1 whole salmon (about 6 pounds)
2 quarts water
1 cup dry white wine
1 cup dry white vermouth
1 large onion, stuck with 2 cloves
2 ribs of celery, cut up
2 carrots, sliced
4 sprigs of parsley

1 bay leaf
6 peppercorns
Slice of lemon
garnish: thin slices of lemon and
    cucumber. Sprigs of watercress
    or parsley
serve with: melted butter, Sauce
    Mousseline, or Sauce Verte

Have the salmon cleaned but not scaled. If you want to serve the salmon with its head on, have the gills removed.

To prepare the court bouillon: combine water, wine, vermouth, vegetables, parsley, bay leaf, peppercorns, and lemon slice in a fish poacher or in a kettle large enough to hold the salmon. Bring to a boil, skim, then lower heat and let simmer for about half an hour. Let cool somewhat.

Wrap the salmon in muslin or in several layers of damp cheesecloth, and lower it into the court bouillon. (If you have cloth hanging over the kettle on both sides, this will facilitate the lowering and lifting of fish. Need we mention that the ends should be short and not hovering near the flame?) Simmer very gently until fish flakes easily when tested with a fork — about 1 hour.

Lift fish carefully from cooking liquid, unwrapping the cloth as you slide it onto a hot serving platter; or cut the cloth when the fish is on platter and gently pull it away. Peel off skin from start of tail up to the head (leaving both tail and head intact) to expose the pink meat on top. Garnish with overlapping slices of lemon and cucumber on top; surround with watercress or parsley. Serve with melted butter or sauce (see following page). Serves 6.

the wine: a dry white Burgundy like Mersault — or a Traminer (from Alsace or California) — or Pouilly Fumé. Or California's Dry Sauvignon Blanc.

serve with: boiled new potatoes. Also buttered green peas and/or a dilled cucumber salad.

See next page for Sauces

Sauces for Whole Salmon au Court Bouillon

Sauce Mousseline: blend ½ cup whipped cream into a cup of homemade mayonnaise or hollandaise.

Sauce Verte: blend finely chopped watercress leaves, parsley, and spinach leaves — or fresh tarragon and chervil if you have them — into homemade mayonnaise.

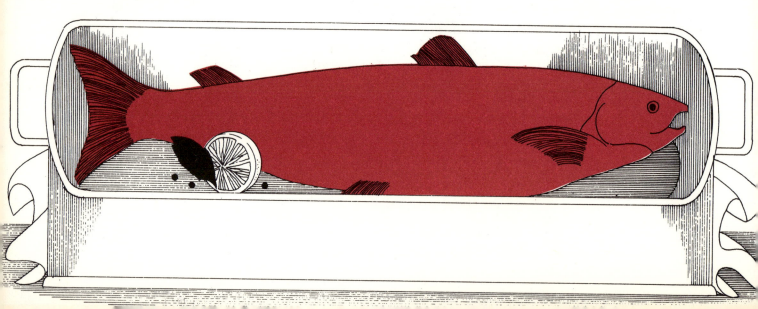

Spaghetti alla Carbonara

1 pound vermicelli (or regular
   spaghetti)
2 tablespoons butter
1 tablespoon olive oil
½ pound smoked ham or thick-cut
   lean bacon, cut in ½-inch
   squares

6 tablespoons dry white vermouth
   or dry white wine
2 eggs, well beaten
¾ cup freshly grated Pecorino,
   Parmesan, or Romano cheese
Coarsely ground black pepper

Put up water in a kettle for the spaghetti (according to label directions) and cook spaghetti until *al dente*. Meanwhile, heat butter and olive oil in heavy skillet and sauté ham or bacon cubes until golden. Remove with slotted spoon and reserve. Add wine to the pan; cook down, and keep hot.

When spaghetti is done, drain well and return to kettle. Add the reserved ham or bacon and the hot wine mixture, and toss. Then add the eggs and cheese; toss again until the egg has coated the spaghetti and is no longer raw. Grind black pepper over all, and serve at once while still hot. Serves 4.

the wine: Chianti

serve with: a tossed salad of lettuce, tomatoes, green and black olives, and rings of mild onion. Or sliced tomatoes, drizzled with olive oil and vinegar and sprinkled with chopped fresh basil. Add a loaf of hot crusty Italian bread if you like. Follow with a fresh fruit dessert — and espresso.

87

Sauerbraten

4 pounds top round or rump of
  beef
1 tablespoon salt
1 teaspoon coarsely ground black
  pepper
2 cups dry red wine
½ cup wine vinegar
2 large onions, sliced
4 ribs of celery, sliced
2 carrots, sliced
1 small lemon, sliced

A few parsley sprigs
2 bay leaves
2 cloves garlic
4 cloves
4 whole allspice
6 tablespoons butter
3 tablespoons flour
2 tablespoons sugar (preferably
  brown)
6 gingersnaps

Three or 4 days ahead: Have your butcher tie up the meat for you. Rub it all over with salt and pepper, and place in a deep enameled, glass, or earthenware crock or bowl. To make marinade, combine wine, vinegar, onions, celery, carrots, lemon, parsley, bay leaves, garlic, cloves, and allspice. Bring to a boil, then pour over the meat. Cover and refrigerate for 3 or 4 days, turning the meat occasionally to make sure it is evenly bathed in marinade.

Lift meat from marinade and pat dry with paper towels. Strain the marinade and reserve. Heat 3 tablespoons of the butter in a heavy casserole or Dutch oven, and brown the meat on all sides. Add the marinade, bring to a boil, cover and simmer gently over very low heat until meat is tender — about 3 hours. Melt remaining butter in a small skillet. Stir in the flour and sugar; cook slowly and stir over low heat until mixture is lightly browned. Add to the casserole, cover and simmer for another 30 to 45 minutes.

Remove meat to carving board or heated serving platter, and slice. Skim fat off cooking liquid. Finely crumble the gingersnaps or grind them in a blender. Stir into the cooking liquid; cook and stir until sauce is thickened and smooth. Pour through a strainer into sauceboat, and serve along with the meat. Serves 6.

serve with: dumplings (especially *kartoffelklösse*, German potato dumplings), boiled potatoes, or buttered noodles. Also cooked red cabbage and butter-sautéed apple slices (or see recipe for Red Cabbage with Apples). Add a loaf of good black bread, if you like. Beer would be the ideal beverage here.

89

Oxtail Ragout

1 large oxtail*
Flour (about 1 cup)
2 teaspoons salt
½ teaspoon freshly ground black
   pepper
¼ cup butter
2 tablespoons olive oil
¼ pound bacon, diced
2 large onions, sliced
6 large carrots, cut in 2-inch
   pieces
2 cloves garlic, minced
Bouquet garni**
2 cloves

Pinch each of rosemary, marjoram,
   and ground mace or nutmeg
2 tablespoons tomato puree
3 cup beef broth
1 cup dry red wine
4 leeks
4 ribs of celery, cut in 2-inch
   lengths
3 or 4 turnips, quartered
¼ cup dry sherry (optional)

garnish: chopped parsley

IN ADVANCE: Have your butcher cut the oxtail into serving pieces. Cover them with cold water and soak for 2 to 3 hours. Drain, cover with fresh water, and bring to a boil, skimming the top. Combine the flour with salt and pepper (either on wax paper or in a large brown-paper bag). Heat butter and olive oil in a large heavy casserole; add bacon pieces and sauté until browned but not crisp. Remove bacon bits with slotted spoon, add oxtail pieces to casserole, and brown. Return bacon to casserole, along with the onions, half the carrots, garlic, *bouquet garni*, cloves, and remaining seasoning, tomato puree, beef broth, and wine. Bring to a boil, then cover tightly, and simmer gently or place in a 300° oven until tender — about 3 hours. Let cool completely, then skim off fat. Discard *bouquet garni*. Refrigerate until about an hour before serving.

Place casserole over a low flame to reheat. Wash leeks thoroughly to remove all the grit. Add to casserole along with the celery, turnips, and remaining carrots. Simmer gently until vegetables are tender. Taste for seasoning. Add sherry (if using), and sprinkle with chopped parsley, if desired. Serves 4 to 6.

the wine: a red Bordeaux or Burgundy. Or California Mountain Red or Zinfandel.

serve with: boiled potatoes or buttered noodles and hot French bread or garlic bread. Add a tossed green salad. If you like, follow with a selection of good cheeses, served with more French bread (with butter) and wine.

*To serve 4 to 6 people, you will probably need at least 4 pounds of oxtail. So if one won't be big enough, buy two, weighing about 2 pounds each. And don't worry about leftovers: this *ragoût* reheats beautifully!

**Bouquet garni:* 4 sprigs parsley, 1 bay leaf, 1 sprig thyme, tied together.

Chicken Cacciatora

¼ cup butter
¼ cup olive oil
 2 chickens (about 3 pounds each), cut up
 2 medium-sized onions, finely chopped
 1 green pepper, thinly sliced
 2-3 cloves garlic, minced
Salt and freshly ground black pepper

 1 can (about 1 pound) Italian tomatoes
 1 teaspoon Italian Seasoning (mixed herbs)
 1 thin strip of lemon peel
 1 teaspoon brown sugar
½ cup dry red wine
Worcestershire sauce

In a casserole or deep heavy skillet, heat the butter and oil, and sauté the chicken pieces until golden brown on all sides. Add onions, green pepper, and garlic (and more oil or butter, if necessary), and sauté until soft. Season to taste with salt and pepper. Mix in the tomatoes (undrained), Italian Seasoning, lemon peel, and brown sugar. Bring to a boil, cover, and simmer over low heat for 30 minutes, stirring occasionally. Add wine and a few dashes of Worcestershire sauce. Simmer for another 15 minutes or until the chicken is tender. Serves 6.

the wine: an Italian red, like Chianti or Valpolicella.

serve with: squares of polenta sautéed in butter and sprinkled with freshly grated Parmesan cheese. If you want to serve a vegetable, broccoli spears would be good here.

93

Lobster Thermidor

4 cooked lobsters (about 1½
   pounds each)*
¼ cup butter
3 tablespoons finely chopped
   shallots or scallions
¼ pound mushrooms, sliced
¼ teaspoon tarragon (optional)
½ cup dry white wine
Salt and white pepper

2½ to 3 cups Rich Cream Sauce
   (see next page)
½ teaspoon dry mustard
Generous pinch of cayenne pepper
   (or a few drops of Tabasco)
Dry sherry
Lemon juice
⅓ cup freshly grated Parmesan
   cheese
2 tablespoons melted butter

Halve the lobsters lengthwise, crack claws, remove lobster meat from shells, and cut into ½-inch cubes. Reserve shells.

Melt butter in a large heavy skillet. Add shallots or scallions, lobster meat,

*If you prefer not to boil the live lobsters yourself, you may purchase them already cooked — as shortly before preparing this recipe as possible. Make certain that their shells are bright red and that the lobsters smell completely fresh; the tail should be curled toward the body and should spring back rapidly when straightened out. This recipe may also be made from cooked (fresh or frozen) lobster meat and served in a baking dish or individual ramekins instead of the shells; allow at least ½ pound lobster meat per person.

and mushrooms; sauté for about 3 or 4 minutes, tossing gently with a spoon. Add tarragon (if using) and wine; season to taste with salt and pepper. Simmer rather vigorously, uncovered, until liquid has almost evaporated.

Add mustard and cayenne or Tabasco to hot cream sauce; season to taste with dry sherry and lemon juice. Fold into the lobster mixture and gently heat through. Spoon into lobster shells, sprinkle with grated cheese, and drizzle with melted butter. Place in a 425° oven or under broiler just until the cheese has delicately browned. Serves 4.

the wine: a dry white Burgundy or a Graves. Or from California, Dry Sémillon or Dry Sauvignon Blanc.

serve with: hot French bread, if desired. Follow with a crisp green salad or a cold vegetable vinaigrette (like asparagus).

See next page for Rich Cream Sauce

RICH CREAM SAUCE: Melt ¼ cup butter in a heavy saucepan, then blend in ¼ cup flour, stirring until smooth. Remove from heat. Gradually add 2 cups milk, then 1 cup heavy cream, blending with a wire whisk until smooth. Return to heat and cook gently, stirring constantly, until sauce is thickened and smooth. Remove from heat, season to taste with salt and white pepper; if desired, add a few grains of grated nutmeg.

Chicken in Champagne

½ cup butter
1 3-pound chicken, cut up
4 shallots, finely chopped
Salt and white pepper, to taste
2 tablespoons flour

1 sprig parsley, coarsely chopped
Pinch of thyme (optional)
1½ cups heavy cream
4 egg yolks
2 cups brut *champagne*

Melt the butter in a heavy casserole. Add chicken pieces and shallots, and season with salt and pepper; turn the chicken a few times. Cover and let cook just barely, over very low heat, for 10 to 15 minutes (the chicken should not brown). Sprinkle chicken with flour, turn again a few times, then pour in champagne and add parsley and thyme (if using). Cover and simmer until chicken is tender. Transfer chicken to a heated serving platter, and keep warm.

Simmer the casserole liquid until it is reduced to about a third of its original amount. Add 1¼ cups cream and continue cooking until reduced by half, stirring occasionally. With a wire whisk, beat together the egg yolks and remaining cream. Add a little of the hot cooking liquid, blend well, then pour into casserole. Cook over very low heat until thickened and smooth; do not let boil. Taste for seasoning, then strain through a fine sieve over chicken. Serves 4.

the wine: Champagne. Or a white Burgundy (like a Corton-Charlemagne) or a Graves.

serve with: steamed rice and, if you like, mushroom caps sautéed in butter. Add a salad of Bibb lettuce and watercress.

97

Shashlik

2 pounds boneless lamb, cut from
    the leg into 1½-inch cubes
Cherry tomatoes
Green pepper, cut in squares
Tiny whole onions (parboiled for
    about 5 minutes)
Mushroom caps

Marinade:
1 cup dry red wine
1 cup olive oil
¼ cup lemon juice
2 teaspoons grenadine (optional)
2 bay leaves
1 large onion, thinly sliced
2 cloves garlic, crushed
¼ cup finely chopped parsley
½ teaspoon oregano
1 teaspoon salt
¼ teaspoon freshly ground black
    pepper

IN ADVANCE: Combine marinade in a large crock or bowl: first beat together the wine, oil, and lemon juice with a wire whisk; then mix in remaining ingredients. Add lamb, cover with a plate, and refrigerate for anywhere from 8 to 24 hours, turning the lamb cubes occasionally.

Alternate marinated lamb cubes on skewers with the vegetables. Grill over charcoal or under hot broiler — turning frequently and basting with marinade

— until meat is crusty brown on the outside but still pink inside (this should take about 10 to 15 minutes). With a fork, push off shashlik onto heated serving plates. Serves 4 to 6.

the wine: a red Burgundy or Bordeaux. Or California Pinot Noir or Cabernet Sauvignon or Gamay.

serve with: a rice or wheat pilaff, saffron rice, or kasha (buckwheat groats). If you'd like a salad, try hearts of lettuce tossed in a lemony vinaigrette dressing (perhaps with some fresh mint leaves added).

Calf's Liver alla Veneziana

½ cup butter
1 ½ pounds calf's liver, thinly sliced
½ teaspoon sugar
¼ teaspoon sage, crumbled
1 pound onions, thinly sliced
⅓ cup flour

½ teaspoon salt
¼ teaspoon freshly ground black pepper
¼ cup dry white wine
3 tablespoons beef broth
2 teaspoons lemon juice
2 tablespoons minced parsley

Melt the butter in a large heavy skillet. Add onions, dust with sugar and sage, and sauté until soft and golden — about 10 minutes. Cut the liver into thin strips (about ⅛-inch wide). Combine flour with salt and pepper on a sheet of waxed paper or in a paper bag; roll liver in mixture, or shake in the bag, until pieces are well coated. Add to skillet and cook over fairly high heat, tossing almost constantly, until browned on all sides — about 3 to 5 minutes. Remove meat and onions with slotted spoon to heated serving platter. Add wine, beef broth, lemon juice, and parsley to skillet. Cook and stir until it comes to a boil, scraping up the crust at the bottom of the pan. Pour over liver and onions. Serves 4 to 6.

the wine: a white Burgundy or Bordeaux, or a dry white Italian wine like Soave. Or California Pinot Blanc.

serve with: steamed tiny new potatoes (unpared) or crisp sautéed potatoes. And hearts of lettuce in oil and vinegar.

Emince of Veal a la Creme

6 slices of cooked veal roast
Salt and white pepper
¼ cup butter
2 tablespoons minced shallots
    (or onion)
1 cup sliced mushrooms

¼ cup dry sherry (or dry white
    wine, or dry white [French]
    vermouth)
½ cup heavy cream
¼ teaspoon lemon juice

garnish: *finely chopped parsley*

Sprinkle veal slices with salt and pepper. Melt butter in a heavy skillet and quickly sauté the veal until golden on both sides. Remove to a heated serving platter and keep warm. Add shallots (or onion) to the pan, along with the sliced mushrooms, and sauté until soft and lightly colored. Add wine and bring to the boiling point. Pour in the cream, and simmer very gently for about 5 minutes, until smooth and thickened. Add lemon juice and taste for seasoning. Pour over veal slices and sprinkle with chopped parsley, if desired. Serves 6.

the wine: a white Burgundy or a Graves. Or, from California, Dry Sauvignon Blanc or Dry Sémillon.

serve with: steamed rice or buttered noodles. Add a fresh vegetable in season (like asparagus or green peas or braised endives).

101

Terrine of Ham Persille

2 cups chicken broth
1½ cups dry white wine
1 teaspoon tarragon
½ teaspoon thyme
1 bay leaf
3 shallots (or a small onion,
  quartered, and 1 clove garlic)

¼ teaspoon peppercorns
2 envelopes (2 tablespoons)
  unflavored gelatin
¼ cup cold water
2 tablespoons tarragon vinegar
1 cup minced parsley
6 cups diced cooked ham

In a saucepan, combine chicken broth, wine, tarragon, thyme, bay leaf, shallots, and peppercorns. Bring to a boil, then simmer for about 15 minutes.

Sprinkle gelatin over cold water, and let stand 5 minutes to soften. Strain the stock mixture through cheesecloth or a very fine sieve. Add a little of the mixture to gelatin and stir to dissolve; then add to remaining stock. Stir in the vinegar and minced parsley. Chill until thickened and syrupy.

Place diced ham in the bottom of a 2-quart casserole or serving bowl. Pour in the stock mixture and return to refrigerator until set. Slice servings directly from the casserole. Serves 6.

the wine: a light white Burgundy. Or Pinot Blanc or Chardonnay from California.

serve with: a mustardy mayonnaise (just add Dijon-style mustard, to taste, to mayonnaise (preferably homemade). Also homemade Melba toast and a mixed green or Caesar salad.

103

Salpicon of Turkey & Ham

3 tablespoons butter
4 shallots (or scallions, white part only), finely chopped
4 cups diced cooked turkey
2 cups diced cooked ham
Salt and freshly ground pepper, to taste
½ teaspoon grated orange peel

½ cup dry white (French) vermouth
1 small can button mushrooms, drained
2 tablespoons slivered blanched almonds
1 tablespoon finely chopped chervil or parsley
Sauce Velouté (see next page)

Melt the butter in a large heavy saucepan or skillet. Add shallots and sauté for a minute or two. Add the turkey and ham, season with salt and pepper, and toss with a fork until heated through. Add the grated orange peel, vermouth, increase heat, and let boil until liquid has almost evaporated. Add mushrooms, almond slivers, and chopped chervil or parsley. Fold in enough Sauce Velouté to bind together all the ingredients and reheat gently if necessary. Serve in flaky pastry shells (use the frozen ones for convenience) or a rice ring.

the wine: California Chenin Blanc.

serve with: buttered petis pois (tiny green peas) or a crisp watercress salad.

Sauce Veloute (for Salpicon of Turkey & Ham)

4 tablespoons butter
5 tablespoons flour
1 cup hot chicken stock
1½ cups hot milk (about)

Salt and white pepper
A few gratings of nutmeg
  (optional)
¼ cup heavy cream

Melt butter in a small heavy saucepan. Stir in the flour and keep stirring over low heat for a couple of minutes. Remove from heat. With a wire whisk, beat in the hot chicken stock, then 1 cup of the hot milk. Return to heat; cook and stir over moderate heat to make a thick sauce, gradually adding remaining milk as needed. Season to taste. Remove from heat and stir in heavy cream.

Chicken Tetrazzini

¼ cup butter
1 cup sliced fresh mushrooms
1 clove garlic, minced
3 to 4 cups diced cooked chicken
¼ cup dry sherry
1 cup Sauce Velouté
(see recipe for Salpicon of Turkey & Ham)
½ cup light cream
2 teaspoons lemon juice

A few gratings of nutmeg (optional)
Salt and white pepper
1 8-ounce package of vermicelli (thin spaghetti), cooked and drained
1 cup hollandaise sauce*
6 tablespoons freshly grated Parmesan cheese

In a large heavy skillet or saucepan, melt the butter. Add mushrooms and garlic and sauté until soft and golden. Add chicken and toss the ingredients with a fork. Stir in the sherry, and cook for another 5 minutes. Stir in the Sauce Velouté, then the cream. Simmer gently (do not let boil!) for 5 more minutes,

*Homemade — or, for convenience, hollandaise is sold in jars in many supermarkets and gourmet-food shops.

stirring often so that sauce does not burn. Add lemon juice, and season to taste.

Place the hot vermicelli in the bottom of a buttered casserole or baking dish. Turn chicken mixture into the casserole, spread hollandaise sauce on top, sprinkle with grated cheese, and place in 400° oven until the surface is golden. Serves 4 to 6.

the wine: some prefer to drink a dry Italian red with this dish (like Bardolino), while others would choose a white (like Soave).

serve with: artichoke hearts or string beans vinaigrette, served after the main course with crusty Italian bread. A nice appetizer for this meal would be chilled melon and prosciutto, served with wedges of lime.

Roast Beef Hash Parmentier

3 tablespoons butter or bacon
    drippings.
1 large onion, finely chopped
½ green pepper, seeded and finely
    chopped
1 clove garlic, minced (optional)
1 teaspoon flour
4 cups diced cooked roast beef
½ cup dry red or white wine

1½ cups beef bouillon
2 tablespoons tomato puree
3 cups diced cooked potatoes
    (another good use for left-
    overs!)
Worcestershire sauce, salt, and
    freshly ground black pepper
2 tablespoons heavy cream
Buttered breadcrumbs*

Heat butter or bacon drippings in a large heavy skillet, and sauté onion, green pepper, and garlic (if using) until soft; sprinkle with flour and toss several times. Add the beef, then stir in wine, bouillon, and tomato puree. Simmer, uncovered, for about 15 minutes, stirring occasionally. Fold in the potatoes, then season to taste with Worcestershire, salt, and pepper. Turn into a buttered casserole or baking dish, drizzle with cream, and top with buttered breadcrumbs. Bake at 350° half an hour. Serves 4 to 6.

serve with: poached eggs, sautéed basil-scented tomato slices, and hot biscuits with honey or marmalade — for a late breakfast.

*Allow about 1 tablespoon melted butter per ½ cup of breadcrumbs.

Old Southern Turkey Hash

6 tablespoons butter
1 tablespoon cooking oil
1 large onion, finely chopped
1 large green pepper, finely
    chopped
4 cups (about) diced cooked roast
    turkey
½ cup (about) cold leftover
    turkey stuffing, crumbled

½ cup blanched almonds, slivered
½ cup finely chopped parsley
Salt and freshly ground black
    pepper
2 tablespoons dry sherry
8 eggs, slightly beaten with 1
    tablespoon cream

Heat the butter and oil in a large heavy skillet. Add onion and green pepper, and sauté until soft. Add the turkey, stuffing, almonds, and parsley; season to taste with salt and pepper, and toss with a fork to mix the ingredients. Then cover for a couple of minutes until contents of pan are hot through. Sprinkle with sherry. Pour in the beaten eggs, and cook and stir over low heat until they are set. Serves 8.

the wine: champagne

serve with: whole hominy (canned), heated with plenty of butter, then drizzled with cream; tiny pork sausages; beaten biscuits. Have fresh-squeezed orange juice in addition to the champagne — and follow with a big pot of hot strong coffee — for a beautiful brunch.

109

Miroton

3 tablespoons butter
1 tablespoon cooking oil
1 or 2 onions, sliced
4 cups (about) of cooked meat
    (beef, lamb, veal, or pork), cut
    in cubes
Salt and freshly ground black
    pepper, to taste
3 tablespoons flour
1½ cups dry red wine
1 can beef bouillon
2 tablespoons tomato paste
1 clove garlic, crushed

1 tiny bay leaf
½ teaspoon basil, rosemary, or
    thyme
Grated peel of ½ lemon
1 teaspoon Kitchen Bouquet
2 tablespoons butter
1 can tiny whole carrots
1 can boiled tiny onions, drained
¼ teaspoon sugar
Lemon juice
1 small can sliced mushrooms

garnish: chopped parsley

Melt 3 tablespoons butter and the oil in casserole, and sauté sliced onions until soft. Add meat, and toss for several minutes, until delicately browned. Add salt and pepper; then sprinkle with flour and toss for a few minutes more, until flour is well blended in. Add wine, beef bouillon, and liquid from the canned carrots and mushrooms. Stir in tomato paste, add garlic, bay leaf, choice of herb, grated lemon peel, and Kitchen Bouquet. Bring to a simmer, then cover and simmer gently for about 45 minutes to 1 hour.

Shortly before serving, heat the 2 tablespoons of butter in a small skillet. Add carrots and onions, sprinkle with sugar and a few drops of lemon juice, and sauté for another minute or so. Gently mix into the ragoût just before taking it off the stove. If desired, garnish with a sprinkling of chopped parsley. Serves 4.

the wine: try one of the California reds, such as Mountain Red or Zinfandel.

serve with: buttered noodles, steamed rice, or boiled or mashed potatoes — and a green salad.

Medaillons of Roast Beef with Sauce Diable

Cooked roast beef
Fine dry breadcrumbs
  2 eggs

2 tablespoons cold water
Butter
Sauce Diable *(see next page)*

Cut roast beef into rather thick rounds.

Pour breadcrumbs into shallow dish or onto a piece of waxed paper. Beat 2 eggs with the water until frothy and lemon-colored. Dip beef slices in crumbs, then into eggs, then again in crumbs. Refrigerate for about half an hour.

Melt butter in frying pan and quickly sauté breaded beef slices until golden brown on both sides and hot through. Serve with Sauce Diable.

the wine: a red Burgundy or Bordeaux, or one of the California reds.

serve with: crisp French fries or corn-on-the-cob. And homemade cole slaw. If you like, add a loaf of hot crusty French bread and an assortment of pickles and olives.

Sauce Diable (for Medaillons of Roast Beef)

2 tablespoons butter
2 shallots (or scallions, white part only), finely chopped
½ cup beef bouillon
½ cup dry red or white wine (or ¼ cup of each)
1 tablespoon Worcestershire
2 tablespoons tomato catsup
¼ teaspoon chervil or thyme

A bit of bay leaf
1 teaspoon dry mustard
½ teaspoon grated lemon peel
1 teaspoon wine vinegar
Dash of Tabasco (or a pinch of cayenne pepper)
1 teaspoon cornstarch
2 tablespoons finely chopped parsley

Melt butter in a heavy skillet or saucepan; add shallots (or scallions) and sauté until golden. Add remaining ingredients, stir well, and simmer for about 15 minutes, stirring occasionally.

Breast of Turkey Divan

2 packages of frozen broccoli
   spears
¼ cup dry sherry
12 thin slices of cooked turkey
   roast
1 cup Basic White Sauce (see
   next page)

2 egg yolks
2 tablespoons butter, softened
¼ cup freshly grated cheese
   (Gruyère or Parmesan)
2 tablespoons whipped cream
2 tablespoons freshly grated
   Parmesan cheese

Cook broccoli according to package directions, and drain well. Arrange the spears in a shallow baking dish and sprinkle with half the sherry. Top with the turkey slices and sprinkle with remaining sherry.

Heat Basic White Sauce in a heavy saucepan, if necessary, over moderate heat. Beat the egg yolks until lemon-colored and stir into the warm sauce (off heat). Then stir in the butter and grated cheese until smooth. Fold in whipped cream. Pour over the turkey, sprinkle with grated Parmesan, and bake at 375° until golden — about 10 to 15 minutes. Serves 6.

the wine: a Beaujolais. Or California's Gamay Beaujolais.

serve with: buttered seashell pasta. Also a green salad, if desired, or
          icy relishes (such as green and black olives, celery hearts,
          cherry tomatoes, scallions).

Basic White Sauce (for Breast of Turkey Divan)

2 tablespoons butter
A few slices of onion
2 tablespoons flour

Pinch each of thyme and grated
  nutmeg
1 cup hot milk
Salt and white pepper

Melt butter in a small heavy saucepan. Add onion slices and sauté until soft. Stir in the flour; using wooden spoon or wire whisk, cook and stir over low heat until well blended. Add thyme and nutmeg. Pour in the hot milk and continue to stir over low heat until thickened. Let simmer for a couple of minutes, stirring constantly. Season to taste with salt and pepper, and strain through a fine sieve. If not using immediately, let cool, then refrigerate in a clean covered jar.

THE WINE CHEF'S
SIDE DISHES & SALADS

Risotto a la Piemontais

3 tablespoons butter
⅓ cup finely chopped onion
1¼ cups raw long-grain rice
¼ cup dry white (French)
  vermouth
2½ cups hot chicken broth

Salt and freshly ground black
  pepper
½ cup freshly grated Parmesan
  cheese
More butter

Melt 1 tablespoon butter over moderate heat, add onion, and sauté until golden. Add 2 tablespoons butter and let it melt. Add the rice and cook, stirring, for a couple of minutes. Add the vermouth and cook until the rice has absorbed it. Add the broth, cover, and let simmer until the rice is tender and has absorbed all the liquid — about 15 minutes. Season to taste with salt and pepper. Add cheese and a lump of butter, and toss lightly with fork. Serves 4.

goes nicely with: chicken; also veal.

If you wish to splurge and make this Rice Pilaff Piedmont-style truly authentic, add a slivered truffle or two along with the cheese. (Truffles, imported in jars from France, are available in most gourmet-food shops and departments.)

Braised Endive au Madere

12 Belgian endives
Salt and white pepper
  5 teaspoons lemon juice
  5 tablespoons butter
½ cup boiling water
  1 carrot, sliced in thin rounds
  1 small onion, thinly sliced and
    separated into rings

Thin slivers of cooked ham (about
  ¼ cup)
Pinch of sugar
¾ cup beef or chicken broth
¼ cup dry Madeira

garnish: chopped parsley

Trim the base of the endives and remove any wilted or damaged leaves. Hold each endive under cold running water, then drain well.

Arrange the endives in a large baking dish or casserole — preferably in a single layer. Sprinkle with ¼ teaspoon salt, a pinch of white pepper, and the lemon juice. Dot with 4 tablespoons of butter, then pour in the boiling water. Cover with casserole lid or aluminum foil, and simmer over moderately low heat for about 10 to 15 minutes. Remove lid or foil, bring to a boil, and cook until liquid is reduced by half. Place a piece of foil or waxed paper directly over the endives, then cover dish with lid or foil. Bake at 350° until almost all the liquid has evaporated and endives are slightly golden — about 1 to 1½ hours.

Melt remaining butter in a skillet or saucepan. Add carrot, onion, and ham, dust with sugar, and sauté until vegetables are tender. Lower oven to 325°. Add broth and wine to skillet, along with any remaining liquid from braised endives, and boil until liquid has reduced by half. Taste for seasoning, then spoon contents of skillet over endives, cover, and bake for another half hour. If desired, sprinkle with chopped parsley. Serves 6.

goes nicely with: chicken and veal, especially. Also chops and roasts.

Spiced Fruits in Port

1 1-pound can dark sweet cherries
1 1-pound can peach halves
1 1-pound can whole peeled apricots
6 thin slices of lemon
1 thin strip of orange peel (optional)

1 1-inch piece of vanilla bean (or ½ teaspoon vanilla extract)
3 whole allspice
¼ teaspoon each grated nutmeg and ground ginger
½ cup port

Drain the syrup from the cans of fruit into a saucepan, reserving the fruit. Add lemon slices, orange peel (if using), and spices. Bring to a boil and let boil, uncovered, until syrup is reduced — about 20 minutes. Add port. Pour over the fruit and let stand for a couple of hours. Then just before serving, return to saucepan and heat through. Serves 8.

Artichokes in Wine

6 artichokes
Acidulated water,* to cover
1 cup dry white wine
3 tablespoons olive oil
1 onion, chopped
1 carrot, chopped

2 cloves garlic, minced
3 tablespoons minced parsley
⅛ teaspoon oregano
Salt and freshly ground black
    pepper, to taste

Cut off artichoke stems so that they can stand upright. Trim off tops of artichokes and remove chokes (the "furry" center core). Wash well under cold running water, then let soak in acidulated water for half an hour.

Drain artichokes and arrange them in a saucepan just big enough to hold them upright. Combine wine, olive oil, vegetables, and seasonings, and pour over artichokes. Bring to a boil, then cover and simmer gently for 45 minutes (or until a bottom leaf pulls out easily) — adding a little more wine and oil if necessary. Remove artichokes to heated individual serving dishes, and pour the hot cooking liquid over each one. Serve as a separate vegetable course. Serves 6.

*Acidulated water: add 1 tablespoon vinegar or lemon juice to each quart of cold water.

Red Cabbage with Apples

1 head of red cabbage (about 3
   pounds)
½ cup butter
4 tart cooking apples
1 very large onion
2 cloves garlic, minced
¼ teaspoon carraway seed,
   crushed
¼ teaspoon each ground allspice,
   cinnamon, and nutmeg
Pinch of thyme

2 teaspoons grated orange peel
Salt and freshly ground black
   pepper, to taste
1 small bay leaf
2 tablespoons brown sugar
2 tablespoons wine vinegar
2 tablespoons red currant jelly
1½ cups dry red wine
2 or 3 tablespoons seedless raisins
   (optional)

Wash cabbage and remove wilted outer leaves. Cut into quarters, remove tough core, and slice into shreds. Melt butter in a saucepan, add cabbage, cover, and cook for 5 minutes.

Peel and core apples and cut into quarters; cut the onion into thin slices. Alternate layers of cabbage, apples, and onion slices in a casserole — beginning with cabbage and ending with apples — until ingredients are used up. Sprinkle each layer with some of the garlic, caraway seed, and remaining seasonings; tuck in the bay leaf. Sprinkle top with brown sugar and vinegar, dot with jelly, and pour wine over all. Cover and bake at 325° until tender — about 2 hours — adding a little more wine or hot water if necessary. If using the raisins, add them to casserole about 10 minutes before removing from oven. Serves 6.

Champagne Dressing for Green Salad

¼ cup brut *champagne (or dry
  white wine)*
6 tablespoons *walnut oil (or
  French olive oil)*

1 teaspoon *lemon juice*
¼ teaspoon *dry mustard*
*Salt and freshly ground pepper, to
  taste*

Mix together all the ingredients until well blended, pour over salad, and toss.

One elegant salad possibility might be Bibb lettuce with a few canned artichoke bottoms (cut into julienne sticks) and a couple of sliced truffles. Or mixed greens — including, perhaps, Boston lettuce, a bit of curly endive, and the Italian arugala (also known here as "rocket"). Or perhaps hearts of lettuce with watercress and sliced avocado.

California Asparagus Salad

About 3 pounds fresh asparagus
   (allow 4 to 6 stalks per person)
Boiling water
Salt
 1 red eating apple
Lemon juice

3 hard-cooked eggs, cut into
   wedges
Pimiento-stuffed green olives,
   sliced
Finely chopped parsley
   6 tablespoons California dry white
   wine

Cut off the tough ends of asparagus stalks, then peel the bottom 2 inches of remaining stalk. Wash well. Arrange the asparagus in a large shallow skillet, add just enough boiling salted water to cover (1 teaspoon salt per quart of water), and cook just until the tips are tender. Drain, cool, and chill.

Just before serving, arrange 4 to 6 asparagus spears on each salad plate. Core the apple, cut into wedges, and brush lightly with lemon juice to prevent darkening. Arrange apple and egg wedges around asparagus. Scatter sliced olives over asparagus, sprinkle with chopped parsley, and drizzle with wine. Serves 6.

This lovely spring salad (which may also be served as a first course) is a special delight to waist-watchers.

Salade Rachel

4 medium-sized cold cooked
  potatoes
4 canned artichoke bottoms
4 ribs of celery
½ cup Sauce Vinaigrette (see
  below)

2 tablespoons port
1 package frozen asparagus tips,
  cooked and drained
2 tablespoons brandy
Mayonnaise (preferably homemade)

Cut the potatoes, artichoke bottoms, and celery into julienne sticks. Mix together the Sauce Vinaigrette, port, and brandy until well blended. Put the vegetables in individual dishes, spoon over a little of the dressing, and let stand for about half an hour. Marinate asparagus tips separately in Sauce Vinaigrette.

Drain the vegetables. Combine the potatoes, artichoke bottoms, celery, and just enough mayonnaise to bind the mixture. Arrange in a mound on serving dish. Garnish with asparagus tips. Serves 4 to 6.

SAUCE VINAIGRETTE (basic French dressing): Blend together 2 tablespoons wine vinegar, ¼ teaspoon salt, and a bit of freshly ground black pepper. Add 6 tablespoons olive oil and beat with fork or wire whisk until thickened.

West Coast Salad

1 head crisp iceberg lettuce
1 tablespoon pear vinegar or
   wine vinegar
Salt and freshly ground black
   pepper, to taste
6 tablespoons salad oil
1 tablespoon dry sherry

4 tablespoons crumbled Roquefort
   cheese
1 avocado
Lemon juice
1 or 2 ripe tomatoes
4 to 6 slices of bacon, fried crisp

Wash head of lettuce under cold running water; let drain for a few minutes, then wrap in paper towels, tie up in a plastic food bag, and refrigerate.

Combine vinegar, salt, and pepper, and stir well; then gradually beat in the oil with a fork or wire whisk. Stir in the sherry, then the Roquefort cheese, and blend well. Taste for seasoning: if you'd like more tartness, add a few drops of lemon juice; if not sweet enough, add a pinch of sugar. Chill well.

Tear or cut the lettuce into bite-size chunks and pile into salad bowl. Peel avocado and discard pit; cut into slices and brush with lemon juice to prevent darkening. Cut tomato into wedges. Arrange tomato and avocado over the lettuce, and scatter crumbled bacon over all. Add dressing and toss. Serves 4 to 6.

THE WINE CHEF'S DESSERTS

Pears a la Bourguignonne

4 ripe firm pears
Cold water to cover, with 1
   tablespoon lemon juice
1½ cups red Burgundy (or other
   dry red wine*)
1 cup water
1 cup sugar

1-inch piece of vanilla bean (or ½
   teaspoon vanilla extract)
1 strip each of orange and lemon
   peel
2 cloves
garnish: sprigs of mint; whipped
   cream flavored with a little
   kirsch

Peel the pears, leaving stems on, and place in acidulated water until ready to use. In a saucepan large enough to hold pears, combine wine and water; bring to a simmer, stir in sugar. When sugar has dissolved, add vanilla, citrus peel, and cloves, and let simmer for about 15 minutes.

Place pears in a small casserole or baking dish, pour syrup over, and bake in 350° oven until pears are just tender (length of time will depend on ripeness of pears) — basting often. Cool the pears in the syrup, then refrigerate. Serve chilled, garnished with fresh mint. If desired, serve with whipped cream that you have flavored with a little kirsch. Serves 4.

*California Mountain Red is excellent for this.

Iced Lemon Souffle with Wine Sauce

1 envelope (1 tablespoon)
   unflavored gelatin
¼ cup cold water
5 eggs, separated
¾ cup fresh lemon juice, strained
Grated peel of 2 lemons

1½ cups superfine sugar
1 cup heavy cream
garnishes: paper-thin lemon slices
   and/or crystallized violets
   and/or sprigs of mint
Wine Sauce (see next page)

Sprinkle gelatin over cold water and let stand for at least 5 minutes to soften. Put the egg yolks into the top of a double boiler; add lemon juice, grated peel, and ¾ cup of sugar. Set over boiling water and cook, stirring constantly, until thickened and custardy. Remove from heat, add gelatin, and stir until dissolved. Chill until a little of the mixture dropped from a spoon forms soft mounds.

Beat egg whites until they start to stiffen. Gradually adding the remaining sugar, continue beating until stiff. Whip the cream until stiff. Fold the egg whites into the chilled lemon mixture, then fold in the whipped cream.

Tie securely a "collar" of double wax paper or foil around the top of a 1½-quart soufflé dish, making sure it stands at least 2 inches above the rim. Pour in the lemon soufflé and chill until firm — about 4 hours. Remove collar and garnish, if desired. Serve with Wine Sauce. Serves 8.

Wine Sauce (for Iced Lemon Souffle)

½ cup superfine sugar
 3 teaspoons cornstarch
½ cup cold water
 2 tablespoons orange juice
 1 tablespoon fresh lemon juice, strained

 1 teaspoon grated lemon peel
 2 tablespoons butter
⅛ teaspoon vanilla extract
½ cup dry white wine
 1 tablespoon brandy

Mix together the sugar and cornstarch in a small saucepan. Add water, orange and lemon juice, and grated peel; stir until smooth. Add the butter and vanilla extract. Bring to a boil, then lower heat; cook and stir for 2 or 3 minutes, until smooth and thickened. Remove from heat, stir in the wine, and chill. Stir in the brandy just before serving.

Peach Melba

4 large, firm, ripe peaches
½ cup dry white wine
½ cup water
1 cup sugar
1-inch piece vanilla bean (or ½ teaspoon vanilla extract)

2 cups fresh raspberries (or 1 package frozen)
½ cup sugar (less if using sweetened frozen berries)
1 teaspoon lemon juice
2 pints vanilla ice cream

Drop the peaches into boiling water for a few seconds; with a fork, dip them into cold water one by one and slip off the skins. (The tip of a sharp knife helps to pierce skin to remove it.) Cut in half and discard pits.

In saucepan, bring wine, water, sugar, and vanilla to a boil, and let boil for a couple of minutes. Add the peaches and simmer gently, uncovered, until tender but still firm. Cool in the syrup, then refrigerate.

Crush raspberries with a fork, add sugar, and chill for an hour or so.

To serve: put sweetened raspberries through a sieve, and stir in lemon juice. Divide ice cream among 8 individual dessert glasses. Top each serving with a drained peach half. Spoon over the raspberry sauce. If desired, top each portion with a spoonful of whipped cream and a sprinkling of shaved almonds. Serves 8.

Figs in Wine & Honey

1 pound fresh (ripe but firm) or
   dried figs
Dry white wine, to cover
½ cup honey

½ teaspoon grated lemon peel
Pinch of cinnamon
Heavy cream

Place figs in saucepan with wine to cover. Bring to a boil, then stir in honey and add grated lemon peel and cinnamon. Simmer, uncovered, very gently until figs are tender. Cool, then chill. Serve with heavy cream. Serves 4.

Compote de Cerises

1–1½ pounds sweet dark-red
  cherries
½ cup dry red wine
½ cup water
½ cup sugar
 1 thin strip of lemon peel

Pinch of salt
 1 teaspoon cornstarch
 1 tablespoon cold water
Kirsch (or other cherry brandy)
  or cognac

Wash the cherries and remove stems and pits.* Tie up several of the pits (about a dozen) in cheesecloth. Combine the wine and water and bring to a simmer. Stir in the sugar; when dissolved, add the bag of pits, lemon peel, and salt, and let boil for about 5 minutes. Add the cherries, cover, and simmer gently until the cherries are just tender — about 10 minutes. Remove cherries to serving dish with perforated spoon and discard bag of pits. Cook the syrup until it is reduced by at least half. Blend the cornstarch with 1 tablespoon cold water, add to the syrup, and cook until syrup is slightly thickened. Remove from heat and flavor to taste with kirsch or cognac. Pour over the cherries, and let them cool in the syrup. Serve warm or chilled. Serves 4.

*To remove pits, the little cherry-pitter gadget (available in many department stores) works nicely. Otherwise, just cut the cherries in half first.

Strawberries Romanoff

2 pints perfect ripe strawberries
Sugar
2 large oranges

½ cup port
Curaçao (optional)
Whipped cream (optional)

Hull the strawberries and place in shallow bowl. Sweeten with sugar if necessary. Squeeze juice from the oranges, combine with the port, and pour over strawberries. Cover and chill for a couple of hours or so. Flavor to taste with curaçao (if using). If desired, serve with whipped cream. Serves 4 to 6.

Zabaglione

6 large egg yolks
Vanilla extract
6 tablespoons superfine sugar

6 tablespoons Marsala (or sweet sherry)
1 tablespoon cognac or brandy

Put egg yolks in the top of a double boiler. With a wire whisk or rotary beater, beat the yolks; add a couple drops of vanilla, then gradually beat in the sugar. Continue beating until mixture is a pale lemon color and thick. Gradually beat in the wine. Place over hot (not boiling!) water and continue beating until mixture foams and coats the back of a spoon. Remove from heat, stir in brandy, spoon into dessert glasses, and serve at once. Serves 4 to 6.

Strawberries Sabayon

2 pints perfect ripe strawberries,
  hulled
The sabayon sauce:
  5 egg yolks
½ cup sugar

1 cup Madeira*
¼ teaspoon grated lemon peel
2 tablespoons cognac or brandy

Beat egg yolks and sugar in the top of a double boiler until lemon-colored and frothy. Heat water in the bottom part of a double boiler until hot, just below the boiling point. Add Madeira and grated lemon peel to egg-yolk mixture. Cook over hot water, stirring vigorously and without pause, until sauce is thickened and foamy. Stir in cognac or brandy. Serve warm or chilled over strawberries. Serves 4 to 6.

*or other sweet wine, such as Marsala, Malaga, port, sherry, Sauternes.

Fruits of the Season Rafraichis

2 pounds fruit in season,*
  quartered, pits removed
½ cup Sauternes (or other sweet
  white wine)
½ cup water
1 teaspoon lemon juice

½ cup sugar (or to taste)
Juice of 1 orange
  2 tablespoons (or to taste)
  curaçao, Cointreau, or Grand
  Marnier

Combine wine, water, lemon juice and sugar in a saucepan. Bring to a boil, lower heat, and simmer for several minutes. Let cool.

Prepare the fruit and place in a serving bowl. Add orange juice, then pour the cool syrup over fruit. Refrigerate until ready to serve, then sprinkle with your choice of liqueur. Serves 8.

*Use an assortment of such fruits as apricots, sweet cherries, nectarines or peaches, plums, seedless grapes. Peel or not, as you prefer. Strawberries and chunks of fresh pineapple would also be good.

English Trifle

1 sponge cake
1 to 1½ cups raspberry jam
¾ cup cream sherry
3 tablespoons brandy
1½ cups custard (your favorite
    recipe or from a mix)

½ pint heavy cream
1 tablespoon powdered sugar
¼ teaspoon vanilla extract

garnish: *a few blanched slivered
    almonds and red currant jelly*

Cut sponge cake into two layers. Spread bottom layer with half of the jam, replace top layer, and cut into 2-inch pieces. Place in a large glass serving bowl. Pour the sherry and brandy over and let soak for about 15 minutes. Spread remaining jam on top, pour cool custard over, and chill for a couple of hours.

Just before serving, whip cream until almost stiff; add powdered sugar and vanilla and whip until stiff. Cover the Trifle with whipped cream, insert a few almond slivers, and dot with bits of jelly. Serves 8.

Fresh Fruit in Champagne

1 large ripe pineapple
1 pint strawberries (hulled) or
   raspberries
4 apricots, quartered

Sugar (superfine or powdered)
  2 tablespoons brandy
  2 teaspoons lemon juice
Chilled champagne

Slice off the top of the pineapple. Then, with a sharp knife, cut out the flesh, leaving a fairly thick shell. Cut the pineapple into neat chunks and combine in a bowl with the other fruit. Sugar to taste, sprinkle with brandy and lemon juice, and toss well. Pile into pineapple shell, and chill. Just before serving, pour in as much champagne as it will hold. Serves 8 to 10.

You may wish to substitute a combination of other fruits—such as apples, plums, pears; melon balls and strawberries; bananas and seedless grapes; strawberries or raspberries and bananas; mandarin oranges (canned) and bananas.

Southern Ambrosia

4 navel oranges
Powdered sugar, to taste
Moist-pack shredded coconut

⅓ cup dry sherry
Whipped cream (optional)

Peel the oranges, making sure to remove the white membrane as well. Cut into thin slices, saving all the juice. In a glass bowl, alternate layers of orange slices (dusting each layer with powdered sugar) and shredded coconut. Sprinkle with sherry and reserved juice from oranges. Chill. Serve with whipped cream, if desired. Serves 4 to 6.

variation: the orange slices may be alternated with layers of sliced bananas, in addition to the coconut, or with fresh or frozen pineapple. (If bananas are used, sprinkle with lemon juice to prevent darkening.)

Wine Jelly

2 envelopes (2 tablespoons)
  unflavored gelatin
1 cup sugar
2 cups boiling water

½ cup orange juice
  2 tablespoons lemon juice
1 cup Madeira, Marsala, sherry,
  or port

Combine gelatin and sugar, add boiling water, and stir until dissolved. Then stir in remaining ingredients. Pour into serving bowl (or a mold that you've rinsed in cold water, to be unmolded just before serving). Chill until set.

If desired, serve with cold custard sauce or whipped cream and/or cut-up fresh fruits.

Serves 6.

Wine jelly also makes a lovely accompaniment to sliced cold turkey, chicken, or ham.

THE WINE CHEF'S GREAT SAUCES

Basic Brown Sauce

¼ cup beef drippings
  1 tablespoon butter
¼ cup each *chopped carrot, onion,*
    and celery
  2 tablespoons flour
  5 cups beef stock

¼ cup tomato paste
Bouquet garni*
  1 clove garlic (optional)
Salt and freshly ground black
  pepper

Melt beef drippings and butter in large heavy saucepan. Add vegetables and cook until soft. Remove pan from heat; add flour and mix well. Cook and stir over *very* low heat until flour is browned (but not burned!). With a wire whisk, gradually stir in the stock and tomato paste; add *bouquet garni* and garlic (if using), and bring to the boiling point over moderately low heat, stirring often. Reduce heat to low and let the sauce simmer until reduced by half. Skim off fat and foam as it rises to the surface during cooking, and stir the sauce once in a while. Season to taste with salt and pepper, and strain through a fine sieve. Yield: about 2½ cups.

NOTE: If not using at once, let cool, then refrigerate in a covered jar. It will keep for several days—or *indefinitely* if boiled up once a week, then refrigerated in a clean covered jar.

Bouquet garni: 3 sprigs parsley, 1 bay leaf, 1 sprig thyme.

The following Great Wine Sauces are based on Basic Brown Sauce, a simplified version of which appears on the preceding page.

Sauce Perigueux

½ cup dry Madeira
 2 cups Basic Brown Sauce
¼ cup smoked ham (preferably
   Virginia), finely chopped
   (optional)

2 truffles, finely chopped
Salt and freshly ground black
   pepper, to taste
2 tablespoons butter

Pour all but 2 tablespoons of the Madeira into saucepan and boil until it is reduced by half. Stir in the Basic Brown Sauce and bring to a boil. Add ham (if using). Cook sauce, uncovered, over low heat for about 15 minutes. Remove from heat. (If you used the ham, strain sauce through a sieve.) Stir in the truffles and remaining wine, season with salt and pepper, then swirl in the butter. Yield: about 1¾ cups.

serve with: roast beef, especially. Also filet mignon, poultry, eggs *en cocotte*, veal.

Sauce Bordelaise

2 shallots (or scallions, white part
   only), minced
Sprig of thyme
1 tiny bay leaf
1 cup red Bordeaux wine

1½ cups Basic Brown Sauce
Marrow from a split beef bone (or
   1½ tablespoons butter)
1 tablespoon minced parsley

Place shallots (or scallions), thyme, bay leaf, and wine in a saucepan; bring to a boil and simmer until reduced by half. Stir in Basic Brown Sauce. Cook over moderately low heat until sauce is reduced to about 1 cup, stirring often. Strain into a clear pan and keep warm.

If using marrow, dice it (using a sharp knife dipped in hot water) and place in a small saucepan; poach it in boiling water for a couple of minutes. Drain well (use paper towels) and add to the sauce just before serving. If not using marrow, add the butter to sauce in bits, stirring briskly with a wire whisk, just before serving. Taste for seasoning and add parsley. Yield: about 1 cup.

serve with: steaks, roast beef, chopped steak. Also good for "dressing up" meatloaf.

Sauce Bigarade

1 tablespoon butter
1 shallot, minced
¾ cup dry red wine
1 tiny bay leaf
1 orange

1 cup Basic Brown Sauce
1 tablespoon red currant jelly
Lemon juice
Curaçao (optional)

Melt butter in a small saucepan or skillet; add shallot, cover, and cook gently for a minute. Add wine, bay leaf, and the peel of half the orange. (When removing peel, take care to use only the colored part of the rind, not the white pith. A vegetable peeler is handy for this.) Simmer until reduced by half. Strain into Basic Brown Sauce, add jelly, and stir over low heat until jelly is dissolved.

Remove remaining peel from orange, cut into very fine shreds; blanch in boiling water for 5 minutes, then drain and add to sauce. Squeeze the juice from half the orange into sauce, and add lemon juice to taste. Simmer gently for about 10 minutes, stirring often. If desired, add curaçao to taste. Yield: about 1½ cups.

serve with: roast duck.

Bigarade is the French name for the Seville (bitter) orange, known to us primarily in English marmalade. As it is hard to come by in this country, the sweet domestic orange has been substituted, with the addition of lemon juice.

Sauce Chasseur

3 tablespoons butter
1 cup sliced or chopped
   mushrooms
1 shallot (or scallion, white part
   only), minced
½ cup dry white wine

1½ cups Basic Brown Sauce
1 tablespoon tomato puree
1 tablespoon finely chopped
   parsley
Salt and freshly ground black
   pepper

Melt half the butter in a saucepan, add mushrooms and shallot, and sauté until mushrooms are soft. Add the wine and simmer until reduced by half. Stir in the Basic Brown Sauce and tomato puree. Simmer gently for about 5 minutes, stirring often. Add parsley and season to taste with salt and pepper. Swirl in the remaining butter. Yield: about 1¾ cups.

serve with: roast or broiled chicken or small cuts of meat (*tournedos,* especially).

Sauce Bearnaise

2 shallots, minced
½ teaspoon tarragon
½ teaspoon chervil
2 peppercorns, crushed
2 tablespoons tarragon vinegar
½ cup dry white wine

¼ cup dry white (French)
   vermouth
3 egg yolks
1 tablespoon cold water
1½ sticks (6 ounces) butter,
   softened
Salt and cayenne pepper
Lemon juice

In a small saucepan, combine shallots, tarragon, chervil, peppercorns, vinegar, wine, and vermouth. Let boil until liquid is reduced by half. Strain into the top of a double boiler, and let cool until lukewarm.

Beat egg yolks with water and add to the liquid in double boiler. Simmer over hot (not boiling!) water, stirring constantly with a wire whisk until light and fluffy. Gradually add the butter, stirring continually with wire whisk, until sauce is thickened. Season to taste with salt, cayenne pepper, and lemon juice. Strain through a fine sieve, and serve. Yield: about 1 cup.

serve with: steaks (classic with *tournedos*) and grilled or baked fish, especially. Also good with broiled or sautéed boned chicken breast, sautéed veal chops or scallopine. Some like it with lamb chops. Often served as one of the dipping sauces for Fondue *Bourguignonne*.

THE WINE CHEF'S CELLAR

The Wine Kitchen

If you prefer not to make a trip to the wine store each time for one or two needed bottles, here is a basic list to start with. It has been stripped to bare essentials and may be revised and added to according to your budget, requirements, tastes. You may, for example, prefer to have two white Burgundies (a Chablis, for instance, and a fuller-bodied one) or to substitute California wines for some of the imports, and so on.

The Wine Chef's Inventory

red wines:
1 bottle Bordeaux
1 bottle Burgundy
1 bottle Rhône (Hermitage or Châteauneuf-du-Pape)
1 Italian (Chianti *classico*)
1 California (e.g., Cabernet-Sauvignon, Pinot Noir, Zinfandel)

white wines:
1 bottle Burgundy
1 bottle Bordeaux (Graves)
1 bottle Alsatian or German
1 California (e.g., Pinot Blanc, Chardonnay, Dry Sémillon,
          Grey Riesling, Johannisberg Riesling, Mountain White)
1 bottle Sauternes (or other sweet white wine)

1 bottle dry white (French) vermouth
1 bottle dry sherry
1 bottle port or Madeira

At the Wine Store

If possible, choose one establishment to patronize and stay with it. By asking around among friends and acquaintances, you will want to locate one which is operated by an able, cooperative, and well-informed wine merchant in whom you can have confidence. In times of doubt, he will be able to advise you — according to your expressed wine-price level, the type of occasion, the dish you are preparing and/or what you plan to serve.

At first, you may want to buy half-bottles instead of whole ones. This will allow for less costly experimentation; half-bottles are also ideal for two or three people at dinner (especially if you plan to serve more than one wine with the meal) and are terrific if you use wine only for cooking and don't want a large opened bottle sitting for weeks in the refrigerator. Then as you begin trying out different wines, you may settle on one or a few special favorites — in which instance, you will find that purchasing wine by the case (12 bottles) is less expensive.

Another good point to remember: do not be swayed by some "famous-name" imported wines being sold at a bargain price unless you know exactly what they are. A good domestic product is often *better* than an inferior European wine, despite the latter's seeming impressive label.

Home Wine Storage

If you have a wine cellar or other suitable storage place, the ideal-temperature consensus is 50° to 55°. The wines must be stored on their sides — so that the cork does not dry out and allow air to seep in (which is *death* to good wine). Specially built shelving is hardly necessary these days with so many types of portable wine racks on the market today — in different sizes to fit personal requirements. And some people even make do with a bookcase or a closet or a bottom bureau drawer! But when storing wine at home, it is important to remember that in addition to the proper temperature, there be as little light as possible — and certainly no bright direct sunlight! If you do not have the correct storage facilities, however, but do purchase wine by the case, ask your wine merchant if *he* will store it (there is a modest annual charge for this service) and allow you to "withdraw" the bottles as needed.

One of the nicest things about wine cookery is that it allows you to use up the remaining dregs in a bottle of wine left over from a dinner party. Who, after all, really has the heart to pour it down the drain?! Here, then, are a few pointers on storing and using *opened* bottles of wine:

1. Apéritif and dessert wines will keep quite well even for weeks if securely recapped and kept in a cool storage spot or, failing that, the refrigerator.

2. Red and white dinner wines are perishable. Even if tightly recorked and

refrigerated, they should be drunk within a day or two of opening. For cooking, remember that it will turn vinegary in a week or two. To help discourage the latter, you may want to decant leftover wine into as small a bottle as possible, then tightly recork it; this way there will be far less air between the wine and the cork.

3. Champagne and other sparkling wines, even if tightly recorked and kept well chilled, will still lose their effervescence. So that it is best to plan on serving them only at the one occasion for which they are opened. *An important note for the wine chef:* without the bubbles, champagne may nevertheless be used in cooking — as a dry white wine.

The Vineyards of Europe

Alsace
Light white wines, inexpensive but nice. Usually named after grapes used, not by area: Riesling, Traminer, Gewürztraminer, Sylvaner, to list the four best-known.
Bordeaux
Regions: Médoc, St.-Emilion, Graves, Pomerol, Sauternes
These regions are then divided into "communes," then into the small elite *châteaux* from whence comes the term "chateau-bottled."
Burgundy
Chablis, Côte de Beaune, Côte de Nuits, Mâcon, Beaujolais
From these districts come several great "estate-bottled" (similar to the chateaux of Bordeaux) wines; several vineyards produce wines that are *not* estate-bottled but regarded with esteem nevertheless.
Loire
Home of three celebrated white wines: Pouilly-Fumé, Sancerre, Vouvray.
Rhône
Home of the great Hermitage and the popular Châteauneuf-du-Pape, two renowned red wines.

GERMANY
Rhine
Rheingau, Rhein-Hesse, the Palatinate
From these regions come such popular white wines as the Rieslings and what we call Liebfraumilch.
Mosel
From this valley come young, delightful white wines.

ITALY
Piedmont: home of Valpolicella, Barolo, Grignolino (reds); the white Soave; Asti Spumante (a sweet champagne).
Tuscany: home of the famed Chianti, the superior version of which is known as Chianti *classico*.
Sicily: source of the celebrated Marsala, a fortified wine.
Turino: vermouth (sweeter than French vermouth).

PORTUGAL
Best known for authentic port (from the city of Oporto), considered by many as the greatest of after-dinner wines. Also home of Madeira from the island of the same name, and two rosé wines that have found many friends in this country: Lancer's and Mateus.

From whence comes true sherry. Also the well-known Rioja wines, both white and red. And Málaga, one of the better-known dessert wines.

For Pot & Palate

LIGHT-BODIED DRY WHITE WINES: Riesling, Sylvaner, some of the Mosels and Rheingaus, Muscadet, Sancerre, Pouilly-Fumé, Soave, Chablis, Neuchâtel. From California: Grey/Johannisberg/Sylvaner Riesling; Pinot Blanc and Pinot Chardonnay.

to go with: *hors d'oeuvres*, oysters, shellfish, lean broiled or poached fish, smoked fish, cold meats (like ham, chicken, turkey), veal simply cooked, *quiche*, sweetbreads, *fettuccine*, light cheese dishes (like a soufflé or fondue).

FULL-BODIED WHITE WINES: the Burgundies (except Chablis), dry Graves, Vouvray, some of the Rheingaus and Mosels (labeled *spätlese*). From California: Dry Sauvignon Blanc, Chenin Blanc, Dry Sémillon, Mountain White.

to go with: poultry, fish, and veal in cream sauces; salmon mousse; chicken livers, liver *pâtés*, rich lobster and crab dishes; pork.

LIGHT-BODIED RED WINES: Bordeaux wines from the Médoc or Graves district; Beaujolais; Bardolino, Valpolicella. From California, Gamay Beaujolais, Zinfandel, Pinot Noir, Cabernet Sauvignon, Mountain Red.

to go with: roast chicken, turkey, duck, lamb, veal, pork; baked ham; stews not made with wine; meat *pâtés*; game birds; soft cheeses (like Brie and Camembert) and the hard ones (like Swiss); steaks simply prepared.

FULL-BODIED RED WINES: Burgundy, Bordeaux (St.-Emilion), Rhône wines (Châteauneuf-du-Pape and Hermitage); Barolo. From California: Ruby Cabernet.

to go with: red meat, hearty red-wine stews and casseroles, games, roast beef, roast stuffed goose; steaks well-seasoned or served with rich brown sauces; kidneys; meats marinated in red wine; strong cheeses (like Roquefort and Gorgonzola).

FORTIFIED & AROMATIC WINES: These sweet wines include port, sherry, Madeira, Marsala, vermouth. The drier versions of which are used in cooking in virtually every course from appetizer to dessert.

SWEET WHITE WINES & CHAMPAGNE: the Sauternes from France is perhaps the best-known of the sweet white wines. (Not to be confused with the domestic sauterne — without the "s" at the end — which is often dry and not to be served as an after-dinner wine.) Champagne is labeled *brut* (the driest), *extra-sec* (extra-dry) and *demi-sec* (semisweet).

Imported & Domestic

When speaking of domestic wines in this book, we have specified the wines of northern California for the reason that they are made from grapes transplanted from Europe, where they have been cultivated for thousands of years. The wines of New York State (the second wine-growing state after California), due to the eastern climate and soil conditions, are made from descendants of *native* grapes and are truly unique, with no European counterparts.* Many people have come to enjoy them for their somewhat "highly flavored" (the experts call it "grapy" and "foxy") taste — while others, long accustomed to European wines, consider them to be lacking the subtlety and other qualities essential to really fine wine.

It is, of course, a matter of personal taste. And for those unfamiliar with our domestic wines — many of which are gaining increasing prestige throughout the world — it can prove to be an exhilarating taste adventure.

*California too produces a few wines which have no European counterparts. Zinfandel is one notable example — a zesty, fruity, informal wine that has found many devoted fans.

Varietal Wines

These wines are labeled according to the variety of grapes from which they were made. For example, the Pinot Blanc grape, grown widely in France, Italy and Germany and used in their dry white wines, lends its name to California's Pinot Blanc (or White Pinot). Cabernet Sauvignon, considered by many to be California's finest, is also the grape used in the red wines of the Bordeaux district of France. Native New York grapes also lend their names to the wine itself — such as Catawba, Niagara, Muscatel, Baco Noir (a hybrid).

For the wine chef who may anguish over the expense or unavailability of a particular European wine — or who simply *prefers* to rely on the domestic ones — it is helpful to know which varietal wines are available as equivalents . . .

	Europe	*California*
RED	Beaujolais	Gamay Beaujolais
	Bordeaux	Cabernet Sauvignon
	Burgundy	Pinot Noir
	Rhône (Hermitage,	
	Châteauneuf-du-Pape)	Petit Syrah

ROSE	Rosé (from Tavel)	Grenach Rosé
WHITE	Burgundy	Pinot Blanc
		Chardonnay
	Bordeaux (Graves)	Dry Sémillon
	Loire	Chenin Blanc
		Dry Sauvignon Blanc
	Riesling	Johannisberg Riesling
	Sylvaner	Sylvaner Riesling
	Traminer	Traminer
	Gewürztraminer	Gewürztraminer
	Sauternes	Sweet Sauvignon Blanc
		Sweet Sémillon

Generic Wines

These are the domestic wines that derive their names from the European wine "types" or regions which they are blended to resemble. Whereas the law requires that varietal wines contain at least 51 per cent of the grape for which they are named, generic wines depend solely on the vintner's formula. Two examples of generic wines are California Burgundy and New York State claret* — which may or may not contain grapes used in the authentic wines of Burgundy

*Claret is the English term for red Bordeaux wine.

and Bordeaux. In the same way, domestic brand-name sherries, port, champagne, etc., are attempted facsimiles of the originals from, in this case, Spain, Portugal, and the Champagne district of France respectively.

Are There Foods That Don't Call For Wine?

As already mentioned, salads, antipasto, vegetables *vinaigrette*, and other dishes made with vinegared dressings. The highly spiced, more "exotic" dishes — like curries, Mexican dishes laden with chili peppers, "hot" Indonesian sambals, etc. — all of which are better off with cold beer. Mint sauce (so frequently served with lamb) and seafood-cocktail sauce will overpower the taste of a good wine. Egg dishes, in general, do not seem to take too well to wine — although a light luncheon of, say, a cheese or country (with potatoes and bacon) omelet, or *piperade basque* (an omelet with onions, green peppers, tomatoes, and ham), would be enhanced by an informal, inexpensive white or red wine. A controversy in gourmet circles continues to be whether or not wine is appropriate for Chinese food: some say that the only acceptable cold beverage with this superlative cuisine is beer, whereas others have ventured out and discovered certain wines to be most complementary.

Improvisations on a Theme

You will find after just a little experimentation that you will be using wine as easily and creatively as you do herbs and spices. The recipes in this book should help to release your creative cooking impulses. Once this is so, you will be surprised and enchanted to learn the innumerable contributions that wine will make to your culinary efforts — from the first course to dessert! Herewith, a few suggestions to help send you on your way . . .

APPETIZERS/SOUPS/SALADS

Next time you serve grapefruit, sprinkle it with sherry in addition to sugar; serve chilled, or place under broiler until lightly browned. Add a little sherry to a seafood cocktail. Add a spoonful of dry wine (white or red) to your salad dressing — or dress potato salad with olive oil, wine vinegar, and white wine instead of mayonnaise. Add a bit of dry sherry, port or Madeira to a clear soup. Flavor carrots with sherry, butter, ground mace, or nutmeg. Same for sweet potatoes and winter squash. Add a few drops of dry white vermouth to creamed onions.

SEAFOOD

Baste fish and shellfish with an equal quantity of dry sherry or dry vermouth and melted butter. Marinate scallops or shrimp in a mixture of olive oil, dry sherry, or dry white wine, and your favorite seasonings before broiling. Steam clams in white wine instead of water. After sautéing fish or shellfish, "rinse" the cooking pan with dry white wine and pour over.

POULTRY

After sautéing chicken, add dry white wine to the pan, stir until it comes to a boil, pour over. Marinate chicken halves in a mixture of soy sauce, dry sherry, ginger, garlic; broil, basting often with marinade. Baste chicken during roasting with a mixture of melted herb butter and dry white wine. Moisten poultry stuffing with a little wine. When roasting a duck or goose, baste with a blend of red Burgundy, orange juice, grated orange rind, a little honey; or use equal amounts of orange juice and port, with a splash of wine vinegar.

MEATS

Add wine to ragouts, casseroles, stews, gravies, sauces. Marinate London broil (flank steak) in a combination of soy sauce, dry red wine, a bit of ginger, garlic, chopped parsley; broil, basting with marinade. After sautéing a steak, add dry vermouth or red or white wine to the pan, along with a lump of butter; blend with pan juices, let sizzle, pour over steak. Do the same with sautéed veal chops and scaloppine, and lamb chops. Baste spareribs with a mixture of dry sherry or madeira, lemon or orange juice, soy sauce, honey. Simmer pork sausages in red wine instead of water. Baste baked ham with champagne or dry white wine and apple juice, or with dry Madeira or sherry. Baste veal roast with dry white vermouth. Marinate meat (beef, lamb, game) in red wine, along with your other seasonings; in addition to adding new flavor enjoyment, wine acts as a tenderizer. Add a little red wine to ground beef (seasoned to taste) before shaping into patties.

FRUITS & DESSERTS

Add white or red wine to water and sugar when poaching fresh fruit. Macerate cut-up fresh fruit in sherry or port, and chill well. Do the same with sugared fresh raspberries and a light red wine. Serve fresh whole peaches (peeled) or strawberries in chilled champagne. Lace custard sauce or softened vanilla ice cream with port, sherry, or madeira, and serve over poached fruit or plain cake. Baste apples with a little dry sherry during baking.

Regional Pairing

You may not wish to "stick to the letter" of the wine chef's code, but a word to the wine-wise on what is *de rigueur* on this important subject is called for. "Regional pairing" is the expression used, and it refers to the practice of preparing and serving a dish which originates from a particular region with a wine from that same region.

For example, Beef *Bourguignonne* would call for a (red) Burgundy. Pasta or meat in a robust Italian-style tomato sauce would be best accompanied by an Italian wine like a Chianti. A *paëlla* would do best with one of Spain's famed Riojas. *Quiche Lorraine* is nicely complemented by an Alsatian (white) wine, as the dish comes to us from the Alsace-Lorraine region. Swiss cheese fondue goes beautifully with Neuchâtel, Switzerland's pleasant white wine. A Riesling or a Rheingau would suit a hearty pork/sauerkraut/potato dish prepared in the German manner. And so on . . .

INDEX

175